M000226288

# Prentice Hall LITERATURE

## PENGUIN  EDITION

# Unit Two
# Resources

*Grade Seven*

# PEARSON

Upper Saddle River, New Jersey
Boston, Massachusetts
Chandler, Arizona
Glenview, Illinois

**BQ Tunes Credits**
Keith London, Defined Mind, Inc., Executive Producer
Mike Pandolfo, Wonderful, Producer
All songs mixed and mastered by Mike Pandolfo, Wonderful
Vlad Gutkovich, Wonderful, Assistant Engineer
Recorded November 2007 – February 2008 in SoHo, New York City, at
Wonderful, 594 Broadway

ISBN–13: 978-0-13-366437-9
ISBN–10:     0-13-366437-6
3 4 5 6 7 8 9 10     12 11 10 09

# CONTENTS

*For information about the Unit Resources, assessing fluency, and teaching with BQ Tunes, see the opening pages of your Unit One Resources.*

## Unit 2: Short Stories  Skills Concept Map—1
## Does every conflict have a winner?

Words you can use to discuss the Big Question

Literary Analysis:
Short Story

A Short Story — has — a plot — and → characters

(demonstrated in this selection)
Selection name:

(demonstrated in this selection)
Selection name:

Reading Skills and Strategies:
Predictions

You can **predict** what will happen next — by — using details in the text and **your prior knowledge** — and by → **reading ahead to verify predictions**

(demonstrated in this selection)
Selection name:

Informational Text:
Magazine Article

You can **examine text features** — to → understand text structure and purpose

**Basic Elements of Short Stories**
• Characters
• Setting
• Plot
• Theme

**Literary Devices**
• Foreshadowing
• Flashback
• Irony
• Dialect

**Comparing Literary Works:**
Character Traits

(demonstrated in these selections)
Selection names:
1.
2.

developed through

indirect characterization

direct characterization

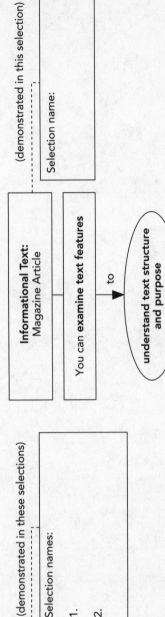
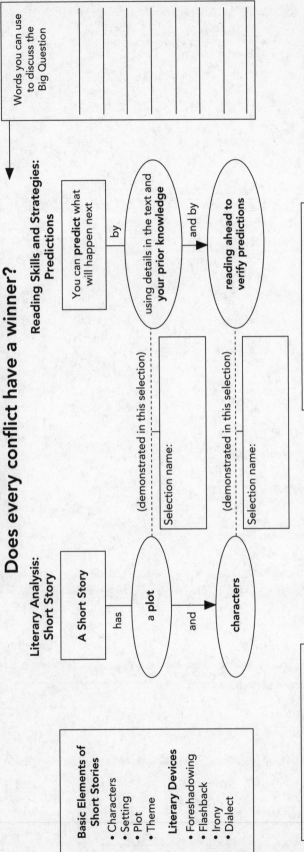

## Student Log

Complete this chart to track your assignments.

| Writing | Extend Your Learning | Writing Workshop | Other Assignments |
|---|---|---|---|
|  |  |  |  |
|  |  |  |  |

# Vocabulary Warm-up Word Lists

*Study these words from "The Treasure of Lemon Brown." Then, complete the activities.*

## Word List A

**brilliance** [BRIL yuhns] *n.* a great brightness
The sun's <u>brilliance</u> filled the room with light.

**commence** [kuh MENS] *v.* to begin
Swimming lessons <u>commence</u> at 9 A.M. tomorrow.

**lifetime** [LYF tym] *n.* the length of time that someone lives
In her <u>lifetime</u>, young Allison had already done many things.

**memories** [MEM uh reez] *n.* the things that one remembers
The family had good <u>memories</u> of their time at the beach.

**swirling** [SWERL ing] *adj.* going in circles with a whirling motion
The <u>swirling</u> top whirled across the floor.

**theaters** [THEE uh terz] *n.* buildings in which shows are presented
Which of the <u>theaters</u> on Broadway is showing a musical comedy?

**throb** [THRAHB] *v.* to beat strongly or fast
When Charles came down with a fever, his head began to <u>throb</u>.

**treasure** [TRE zher] *n.* something very special or valuable
To Peter, the rocks he collects are a <u>treasure</u>.

## Word List B

**awaited** [uh WAY tid] *v.* was in store for
The assignment, put off all weekend, <u>awaited</u> Michelle.

**beckoned** [BEK uhnd] *v.* called with a silent motion
Diana <u>beckoned</u> to me with her right hand.

**brittle** [BRIT uhl] *adj.* having a hard, sharp quality
The old recordings were marked by <u>brittle</u>, scratching sounds.

**lecturing** [LEK cher ing] *v.* giving a lengthy scolding
When Trevor gets home late, his parents are soon <u>lecturing</u> him.

**ominous** [AHM uh nuhs] *adj.* threatening; like an evil sign
The scary decorations in the Fun House gave it an <u>ominous</u> look.

**revealed** [ri VEELD] *v.* made known something that was hidden
Jeremy <u>revealed</u> his sister's gift, which was hidden in the closet.

**suspense** [suh SPENS] *n.* a state of nervous uncertainty
The <u>suspense</u> of not knowing who would win the contest was almost too great to bear.

**youngster** [YUHNG ster] *n.* a child or young person
The <u>youngster</u> spent his mornings at a day-care center.

**"The Treasure of Lemon Brown"** by Walter Dean Myers
# Vocabulary Warm-up Exercises

**Exercise A** *Fill in each blank in the paragraph below with an appropriate word from Word List A. Use each word only once.*

Marissa loved going to [1] _____ to see live shows. To her those outings were a [2] _____, a most valuable experience. She felt a thrill as the curtain rose and the play would [3] _____. If there was music, the beat of the drums might [4] _____. Dancers would whirl around, the women's [5] _____ skirts creating a flash of [6] _____ under the spotlights. For Marissa, nothing compared with live performances. Although she was only fifteen, she felt she had lived a [7] _____. She would cherish her [8] _____ for years to come.

**Exercise B** *Answer each question in a complete sentence. Use a word from Word List B to replace each underlined word or group of words without changing the meaning.*

**Example:** What kind of situation might require you to act gently and sensitively? (delicately) *I would act delicately if I had to give someone bad news.*

1. What threatening thing might have been in store for someone at one time?
   _____
   _____

2. Has anyone ever summoned you with a signal?
   _____

3. Have you ever read a story that kept you feeling anxious excitement until the identity of the villain was disclosed?
   _____
   _____

4. Does the hard, sharp noise of chalk scratching the blackboard ever bother you?
   _____

5. When might someone be giving a child a lengthy scolding?
   _____

6. How does a child spend his or her time?
   _____

___ 8. Why does Greg enter the building where Lemon Brown is staying?
   **A.** He is curious about Lemon Brown's treasure.
   **B.** He knows his father will lecture him when he goes home.
   **C.** He wants to join the checkers tournament.
   **D.** He wants to avoid some thugs who are on the sidewalk.

___ 9. Lemon Brown says, "Every man got a treasure. You don't know that, you must be a fool!" What aspect of the story is brought out by those lines?
   **A.** the setting
   **B.** direct characterization
   **C.** the theme
   **D.** the conflict

___ 10. What conflict do Greg and Lemon Brown share?
   **A.** They fear they will lose their treasure.
   **B.** They must find a safe place to live.
   **C.** They must face a group of thugs.
   **D.** They have lost people they loved.

___ 11. The climax of the story occurs when
   **A.** Greg learns that Lemon Brown's treasure is a harmonica.
   **B.** Greg decides not to tell his father about Lemon Brown.
   **C.** one of the thugs starts climbing the stairs toward Lemon Brown.
   **D.** Greg howls, and Lemon Brown hurls himself down the stairs.

___ 12. What motivates the thugs?
   **A.** They think that Lemon Brown's treasure is worth a lot of money.
   **B.** They know that Lemon Brown was once a famous blues singer.
   **C.** They believe that Lemon Brown has reported them to the police.
   **D.** They think that Lemon Brown's harmonica is made of solid gold.

___ 13. Lemon Brown gave the harmonica and news clippings to his son because he wanted his son to
   **A.** become a great blues singer.
   **B.** guard his treasure.
   **C.** return from the war safely.
   **D.** know about his father's achievements.

___ 14. Lemon Brown tells Greg that his heart was broken when
   **A.** he found out that his son had been killed in the war.
   **B.** he found out that his son did not appreciate his treasure.
   **C.** he realized that he was not talented enough to be a great blues singer.
   **D.** he realized that his son did not value the harmonica as much as he did.

___ 15. Lemon Brown is surprised and pleased to learn that
   **A.** Greg was interested in learning to play the harmonica.
   **B.** Jesse was going to find a place for him to live in East St. Louis.
   **C.** Jesse treated the harmonica and clippings as if they were treasures.
   **D.** Greg was going to try to do better in math so that he could play basketball.

___ 16. Lemon Brown tells Greg about Jesse during the story's
    A. exposition.
    B. rising action.
    C. falling action.
    D. resolution.

___ 17. During the story, Greg's feelings for Lemon Brown change from
    A. fear to curiosity to respect.
    B. curiosity to horror to acceptance.
    C. fear to friendship to alarm.
    D. concern to fear to friendship.

___ 18. Which statement is true of "The Treasure of Lemon Brown"?
    A. Most of the action takes place on a city street.
    B. Most of the action takes place inside an abandoned building.
    C. Most of the action takes place in Greg's apartment.
    D. Most of the action takes place early in the Community Center.

___ 19. Greg most likely decides not to tell his father about Lemon Brown because
    A. he does not want to get a lecture about being out after dark on a school night.
    B. he is afraid that his father will think Lemon Brown's treasure is silly.
    C. he wants to help Lemon Brown find a new place to live.
    D. he wants to respect Lemon Brown's privacy.

___ 20. Which statement best expresses the theme of "The Treasure of Lemon Brown"?
    A. The life of a blues singer can be extremely difficult.
    B. People should respect what their fathers say and do.
    C. The value of a treasure may be unrelated to its monetary value.
    D. To play sports, you must work hard in school and get good grades.

**Essay**

21. In an essay, discuss what Greg learns about fathers from Lemon Brown. Consider how that lesson might affect Greg's relationship with his own father. Support your points by citing at least two details from "The Treasure of Lemon Brown."

22. In an essay, state what you think is the theme of "The Treasure of Lemon Brown." Support your opinion by citing at least two details from the story. Then, tell whether or not the theme you stated is a universal theme, and explain why it is or is not.

23. A character's traits—revealed through his appearance, words, and actions—help readers understand the character and his or her actions. A character acts in certain ways because of his or her motives. In an essay, discuss what Lemon Brown's character traits tell you about him and his actions. Tell what motives lead him to act as he does.

24. **Thinking About the Big Question: Does every conflict have a winner?** Write an essay in which you describe two of the conflicts in the story. Explain whether each conflict has a winner and, if it does, who the winner is. Cite details from the story to support your points.

# Vocabulary Warm-up Word Lists

*Study these words from "The Bear Boy." Then, apply your knowledge in the activities that follow.*

## Word List A

**lance** [LANS] *n.* a long spear
   The knight aimed the deadly lance at his enemy.

**lodge** [LAHJ] *n.* a small house
   Kuo-Haya lived in an adobe lodge built into the mountainside.

**neglected** [ni GLEKT id] *v.* failed to do something
   Sara neglected to water her plants, so they soon wilted.

**preparations** [prep uh RAY shunz] *n.* the work involved in making something ready
   The preparations for the wedding included choosing flowers.

**result** [ri ZUHLT] *n.* something that happens because of something else
   As a result of the new policy, students can take classes online.

**timid** [TIM id] *adj.* shy; not brave or confident
   Cameron felt timid when he spoke before a large audience.

**weapons** [WEP uhnz] *n.* things used to fight with
   International law prohibits the use of nuclear weapons.

**wrestling** [RES ling] *adj.* struggling and holding
   The children wrestling outside are just playing.

## Word List B

**encourage** [en KUR ij] *v.* to support and give confidence
   My parents encourage me to pursue my dreams.

**guidance** [GY duhns] *n.* helpful advice or counsel
   Ms. Tillman's students seek her guidance when they want to improve their grades.

**initiation** [i nish ee AY shun] *n.* introduction into a group or club
   The new members prepared for their initiation into the fellowship.

**manhood** [MAN hood] *n.* the state of being an adult man rather than a boy
   Mark felt he had entered manhood when he took over the family business.

**powerful** [POW er fuhl] *adj.* having great strength or authority
   The singer's powerful voice was heard clearly in the last row of the huge auditorium.

**relatives** [REL uh tivz] *n.* members of your family
   Aunt Mary and Uncle John are my favorite relatives.

**responsibility** [ri spahn suh BIL uh tee] *n.* a duty or job
   Logan accepted the responsibility of being class president.

**violence** [VY uh luhns] *n.* physical force that is capable of hurting others
   Disagreements that become physical result in violence.

**"The Bear Boy"** by Joseph Bruchac
# Vocabulary Warm-up Exercises

**Exercise A** *Fill in each blank in the paragraph below with an appropriate word from Word List A. Use each word only once.*

The abandoned building had once been a replica of an adobe [1] _____.
The money to maintain it had run out. As a [2] _____, it had been
[3] _____ for years. Inside on a worn blanket lay someone's
[4] _____ for a meal, the food now covered in dust. The collection of
[5] _____ hanging on the wall, including a [6] _____,
seemed out of place. The Pueblos were not a [7] _____ people, but neither were they warriors. On one wall hung pictures of Pueblo children
[8] _____ with one another.

**Exercise B** *Answer the questions with complete explanations.*

**Example:** If a person acts <u>immaturely</u>, is he or she acting like an adult?
*No; <u>immaturely</u> means "lacking the characteristics of an adult," so someone who is acting immaturely is not acting like an adult.*

1. When you <u>encourage</u> someone, are you being helpful?
   _____

2. If you view a scene of <u>violence</u>, is it a pleasant sight?
   _____

3. When you go through an <u>initiation</u> into a club, have you become a member of the club?
   _____

4. Do a person's <u>relatives</u> include everyone in his or her neighborhood?
   _____

5. If you fulfill a <u>responsibility</u>, are you likely to feel good about what you have done?
   _____

6. If someone has a <u>powerful</u> personality, would he or she stand out in a group?
   _____

7. Do boys enter <u>manhood</u> when they graduate from fifth grade?
   _____

8. Would you be pleased if someone offered you <u>guidance</u>?
   _____

# Vocabulary Warm-up Word Lists

*Study these words from "Rikki-tikki-tavi." Then, complete the activities.*

## Word List A

**balancing** [BAL uhns ing] *v.* keeping steady and not falling over
The acrobat was <u>balancing</u> a chair on his chin.

**bred** [BRED] *v.* raised
Ms. Cochrane <u>bred</u> English terriers for show.

**brood** [BROOD] *n.* all the young in one family
The hen led her <u>brood</u> of chicks into the barn.

**clenched** [KLENCHT] *v.* held or squeezed
Chelsea <u>clenched</u> the bat and swung hard at the fast ball.

**fraction** [FRAK shuhn] *n.* a small portion or small amount
At discount stores, you may pay a <u>fraction</u> of an item's value.

**peculiar** [pi KYOOL yer] *adj.* strange or odd
The strangely dressed performers were a <u>peculiar</u> sight.

**splendid** [SPLEN did] *adj.* beautiful or impressive; brilliant
From the mountaintop at dawn, we saw a <u>splendid</u> sunrise.

**thickets** [THIK its] *n.* thick growths of plants or bushes
The rabbit hid in the <u>thickets</u> that grew along the trail.

## Word List B

**bungalow** [BUHNG uh loh] *n.* a small house
The <u>bungalow</u> was large enough to house just the two of them.

**inherited** [in HER it id] *v.* received a trait or possession passed down by one's family
My brothers and I <u>inherited</u> our mother's long, straight nose.

**paralyzed** [PA ruh lyzd] *v.* made someone or something helpless and unable to function
The venom of the black mamba temporarily <u>paralyzed</u> its prey.

**revived** [ri VYVD] *v.* brought someone or something back to consciousness
The paramedic <u>revived</u> the accident victim.

**savagely** [SAV ij lee] *adv.* fiercely; violently
The lion roared <u>savagely</u> before disappearing into the jungle.

**scornfully** [SKAWRN fuh lee] *adv.* expressing something in a way that shows dislike or disrespect
The unhappy employee spoke <u>scornfully</u> of the new manager.

**scuttled** [SKUHT uhld] *v.* ran or moved quickly with short steps
The little dog <u>scuttled</u> across the slippery floor.

**valiant** [VAL yuhnt] *adj.* brave or courageous
We honor the country's <u>valiant</u> soldiers on Veteran's Day.

**"Rikki-tikki-tavi"** by Rudyard Kipling
# Vocabulary Warm-up Exercises

**Exercise A** *Fill in each blank in the paragraph below with an appropriate word from Word List A. Use each word only once.*

The fox led her [1] _____ of pups into the den before returning to the riverbank. She smelled a [2] _____ odor. It was odd—not the odor of another animal. She was [3] _____ to be cautious, so she stayed deep in the [4] _____, well out of sight. Soon she saw a boy. He was [5] _____ on a stone as he tried to cross the narrow river. He [6] _____ a fishing rod tightly in one hand. The fox slunk back just a [7] _____ of an inch and then turned and ran. The boy caught sight of the impressive animal. "What a [8] _____ fox!" he cried just as he lost his footing and splashed into the river.

**Exercise B** *Answer the questions with complete explanations.*

**Example:** If you are <u>hurrying</u>, are you taking your time?
*No; <u>hurrying</u> means "rushing," so I would not be taking my time.*

1. If someone spoke <u>scornfully</u> to you, would you be pleased?
   _____

2. If you <u>inherited</u> your father's looks, would you resemble your father?
   _____

3. If your jaw were <u>paralyzed</u>, would you be able to open your mouth?
   _____

4. If you lived in a <u>bungalow</u>, would you have room for a lot of guests?
   _____

5. If a friend did something <u>valiant</u>, would you admire her?
   _____

6. If someone <u>scuttled</u> away, would you think he or she was in no hurry?
   _____

7. If the wind was said to be blowing <u>savagely</u>, would you go outside?
   _____

8. If someone has been <u>revived</u>, is he or she asleep?
   _____

**"Rikki-tikki-tavi"** by Rudyard Kipling
# Reading Warm-up A

*Read the following passage. Pay special attention to the underlined words. Then, read it again, and complete the activities. Use a separate sheet of paper for your written answers.*

The Indian mongoose has a splendid reputation for bravery. That reputation dates back to ancient Egypt, where the weasel-like creature scouted out crocodiles and ate their eggs or their newly hatched brood. The ancient Egyptians called the mongoose pharaoh's mouse, but that name is misleading. The mongoose is no mouse.

The Indian mongoose lives in fields or in heavy brush: tangled thickets and hedges. It eats rats, mice, snakes, lizards, the eggs of those creatures, and insects. It usually hunts at night. Most important, the mongoose can move like lightning. Its speed is a great advantage when it does the thing for which it is most famous: killing cobras and other snakes native to India. The mongoose is a snake's worst enemy.

In some ways the mongoose has an advantage over the snake. Its thick hide and long thick hair act as armor, protecting it from the snake's poisonous fangs. In addition, it takes a lot of cobra venom to kill an adult mongoose. The young mongoose is at risk, however, because its body is less tolerant of the venom. Many young mongooses die of snakebites before they can become skilled fighters.

The mongoose's snake dance is dazzling to behold. The mongoose is balancing lightly on its feet. In a fraction of a second, it leaps in any direction. By the time the snake strikes, the mongoose has already moved. When the snake grows exhausted, the mongoose leaps onto its back. At last the mongoose has clenched the snake's head between its sharp teeth, and it snaps the snake's spine.

Some species of mongooses are bred as pets. A mongoose may seem like a peculiar pet, but the animal is both intelligent and entertaining. If you happen to be in India, one may even save your life.

1. Underline the words that tell what is splendid about the mongoose. Give an antonym of *splendid*.

2. Circle the words that describe the crocodiles' brood. In your own words, rewrite the sentence, using a synonym for *brood*.

3. Circle the words that give a clue to the meaning of thickets. Use *thickets* in a sentence.

4. Underline the words that tell how the mongoose is balancing. Define *balancing*.

5. Underline the words that tell what happens in a fraction of a second. Tell about something else that can happen in a *fraction* of a second.

6. Circle the words that tell what the mongoose has clenched between its teeth. Rewrite the sentence, using a synonym for *clenched*.

7. Circle the words that tell what some mongooses are bred for. Name another animal that is *bred* for a special purpose.

8. Circle the words that tell what may seem like a peculiar pet. Write a sentence explaining why it is not really *peculiar*.

**"Rikki-tikki-tavi"** by Rudyard Kipling
# Reading Warm-up B

*Read the following passage. Pay special attention to the underlined words. Then, read it again, and complete the activities. Use a separate sheet of paper for your written answers.*

Heather was <u>paralyzed</u> by the heat and humidity. She could not move, so she sat on the porch of the <u>bungalow</u>, sipping lemonade while the sun's heat beat <u>savagely</u> down on the tile roof. The doors and windows stood wide open, welcoming every wayward breeze. That did not help much, though. There was hardly a breath of air. Occasionally, a beetle <u>scuttled</u> across the porch, but mostly the insects remained silent and still in the heat of the burning sun.

"So this is India," thought Heather.

The bungalow in which she was staying belonged to her grandparents. Three days before, she had arrived for a month-long vacation. The house was near Calcutta, India's largest city, a teeming hive of activity. Heather had never been to India before, but she had <u>inherited</u> her grandfather's love of travel. She longed to see it all, from the parched desert to the snow-covered mountains. Still, she knew that the country was too vast to be seen in a lifetime, let alone a month's vacation.

Heather's family had lived here for generations. They had lived here when Great Britain ruled the country. Those days were long over, however. India gained its independence in the 1940s, after a <u>valiant</u> struggle against colonial rule. Many British politicians had <u>scornfully</u> predicted that India would not be able to rule itself, but they were wrong. The country is strong and thriving. Now the British return as guests, not as rulers.

Heather gazed from the porch that encircled the house, watching dark clouds blowing in from the Bay of Bengal. It would start to rain soon. Just the thought of rain <u>revived</u> her energy. Perhaps she would drive to Calcutta and explore the city. It was time to learn more, to see more.

1. Tell what <u>paralyzed</u> Heather. Circle the words that give the meaning of *paralyzed*.

2. Circle the phrase that tells where in the <u>bungalow</u> Heather is sitting. Write a sentence describing where you might see a *bungalow*.

3. Tell what beat <u>savagely</u> down on the roof. Use *savagely* in a sentence of your own.

4. Circle the word that tells what kind of insect <u>scuttled</u> across the porch. What is a synonym for *scuttled*?

5. Underline the phrase that tells what Heather <u>inherited</u>. Name something else that might be *inherited*.

6. Circle the word that tells what India gained after a <u>valiant</u> struggle. Write the meaning of *valiant*.

7. Underline the words that tell what was <u>scornfully</u> predicted. Use *scornfully* in a sentence.

8. Circle the words that tell what <u>revived</u> Heather's energy. Tell what has *revived* your energy on a hot day.

## Essay

*Write an extended response to the question of your choice or to the question or questions your teacher assigns you.*

11. Consider the five basic plot elements in a story: exposition, rising action, climax, falling action, and resolution. In an essay, describe an event in "Rikki-tikki-tavi" that illustrates each element. Explain how each event contributes to the story as a whole.

12. Did you predict the outcome of the battle between Rikki-tikki and Nagaina? In an essay, explain how easy or difficult it is for readers to predict the outcome of "Rikki-tikki-tavi." What prior knowledge do they need? What events in the story help the reader predict the outcome?

13. "Rikki-tikki-tavi" is a story of conflict between natural enemies. The animals have personalities and character traits that are very human. In an essay, analyze how traits such as loyalty, bravery, and selfishness move the story forward. Illustrate your points with examples of events in the story.

14. **Thinking About the Big Question: Does every conflict have a winner?** In "Rikki-tikki-tavi," there are some very clear winners and losers. In an essay, explain who wins and who loses in the story. Then, explain how the clarity of the conflict's outcome might contribute to the story's lasting popularity.

## Oral Response

15. Go back to question 1, 6, or 8 or to the question your teacher assigns you. Take a few minutes to expand your answer and prepare an oral response. Find additional details in "Rikki-tikki-tavi" that will support your points. If necessary, make notes to guide your response.

**"Rikki-tikki-tavi"** by Rudyard Kipling
# Selection Test A

**Critical Reading** *Identify the letter of the choice that best answers the question.*

____ 1. What kind of animal is Rikki-tikki-tavi?
  **A.** a cat
  **B.** a muskrat
  **C.** a weasel
  **D.** a mongoose

____ 2. In "Rikki-tikki-tavi," a flood takes Rikki-tikki from his home to the care of an English family. In what part of the plot does the flood take place?
  **A.** during the climax
  **B.** during the resolution
  **C.** during the falling action
  **D.** during the exposition

____ 3. Based on this quotation and your prior knowledge, what can you predict will happen?
  "No," said his mother; "let's take him in and dry him. Perhaps he isn't really dead."
  **A.** Rikki-tikki will soon die.
  **B.** Rikki-tikki will probably live.
  **C.** The mother will become Rikki-tikki's only friend.
  **D.** Rikki-tikki will fight Nag and Nagaina.

____ 4. At the beginning of "Rikki-tikki-tavi," which characteristic does Rikki-tikki display as soon as he has warmed up?
  **A.** greed
  **B.** bravery
  **C.** curiosity
  **D.** laziness

____ 5. Based on the following passage, what do you think it means when the tail of an animal like Rikki-tikki grows "bottlebrushy"?
  "This is a splendid hunting ground," [Rikki-tikki] said, and his tail grew bottlebrushy at the thought of it.
  **A.** The animal is happy and excited.
  **B.** The animal is hungry.
  **C.** The animal is lost and afraid.
  **D.** The animal is alert.

_____ 6. When Rikki-tikki first comes to the garden, a conflict is introduced. Whom is the conflict between?
   A. Nag and Nagaina
   B. Rikki-tikki and Nag
   C. Rikki-tikki and Darzee
   D. Darzee and Darzee's wife

_____ 7. Who is Nagaina?
   A. Nag's wife
   B. Nag's father
   C. Nag's sister
   D. Nag's mother

_____ 8. After Rikki-tikki kills Karait, how does he feel?
   A. confident
   B. annoyed
   C. jealous
   D. defeated

_____ 9. What prediction can you make based on your prior knowledge and this quotation from "Rikki-tikki-tavi"?

   "Teddy's safer with that little beast than if he had a bloodhound to watch him. If a snake came into the nursery now—"

   A. The snakes are not a threat to Teddy.
   B. Rikki-tikki will fail to protect Teddy from a snake attack.
   C. Rikki-tikki will protect Teddy from a snake attack.
   D. Rikki-tikki will attack Teddy.

_____ 10. The birds and frogs rejoice and sing, "Ding-dong-tock! Nag is dead!" In what part of the plot does this event take place?
   A. during the rising action
   B. during the falling action
   C. during the exposition
   D. during the climax

_____ 11. Which statement best describes Rikki-tikki's character?
   A. He is cautious and selfish.
   B. He is fierce and bloodthirsty.
   C. He is brave and loyal.
   D. He is loving and shy.

## Vocabulary and Grammar

____ 12. In which sentence about "Rikki-tikki-tavi" is *immensely* used correctly?

    A. Darzee's wife takes great pride in her immensely eggs and cares for them.

    B. Once Teddy's family gets used to living in the bungalow, they like it immensely.

    C. The Coppersmith, the town crier of every garden, spreads the word immensely.

    D. Fearful that Nagaina will turn and strike at him, Rikki-tikki holds on immensely.

____ 13. In which sentence about "Rikki-tikki-tavi" is *revived* used correctly?

    A. The garden Rikki-tikki entered revived lime and orange trees.

    B. Teddy's father revived Nag by shooting him with his rifle.

    C. Teddy's family was revived to know that Nagaina was dead.

    D. After Rikki-tikki revived, he thought how lucky he was to be alive.

____ 14. Which word in this passage is a linking verb?

    Teresa was on the phone when Megan arrived to pick her up.

    A. was                    C. arrived

    B. when                D. pick

____ 15. Which word in this passage from "Rikki-tikki-tavi" is an action verb?

    "Who is Nag?" he said. "*I* am Nag."

    A. Who                  C. said

    B. is                    D. am

## Essay

16. Did you predict the result of the battle between Rikki-tikki-tavi and Nagaina? In an essay, explain how easy or difficult it is for readers to predict the outcome of "Rikki-tikki-tavi." Name the events in the story that might help the reader predict the outcome. Name any events that might make it difficult for the reader to predict the outcome.

17. Consider the five basic plot elements: exposition, rising action, climax, falling action, and resolution. In an essay, describe an event in "Rikki-tikki-tavi" that illustrates each element. Then, explain why you think the plot elements do or do not create a satisfying story.

18. **Thinking About the Big Question: Does every conflict have a winner?** In "Rikki-tikki-tavi," there are some very clear winners and losers. In an essay, explain who wins and who loses. Then, discuss how the conflict's outcome might explain the story's lasting appeal to readers.

## Essay

*Write an extended response to the question of your choice or to the question or questions your teacher assigns you.*

11. Rifka's life is about to change completely. In an essay, describe three ways in which her life may be different once the family arrives in America. Base your predictions on what the story reveals about Rifka's character and the situation her family faced while in Russia.

12. Rifka and Nathan are about to face the challenges and hardships of a long, dangerous trip to a distant land. In an essay, discuss how their character traits will affect their chances of making it safely to America. Which traits do they share? How will their character traits help them? Use examples from *Letters from Rifka* to support your answer.

13. Rifka and her family are facing the difficult task of leaving their homeland and journeying thousands of miles to a faraway country about which they know very little. Based on what you read about conditions in Russia at the time, why would Rifka's family want to make such a long, difficult journey? What will they lose? What problems and opportunities likely await them in America? Discuss these issues in an essay, supporting your answer with concrete examples.

14. **Thinking About the Big Question: Does every conflict have a winner?** Think about the main conflict in *Letters from Rifka*. Write an essay explaining the conflict. Who is involved in it? Who is the winner? What would have happened if the other side had won?

## Oral Response

15. Go back to question 2, 3, or 7 or to the question your teacher assigns you. Take a few minutes to expand your answer and prepare an oral response. Find additional details in *Letters from Rifka* that will support your points. If necessary, make notes to guide your response.

*from* **Letters from Rifka** by Karen Hesse
## Selection Test A

**Critical Reading** *Identify the letter of the choice that best answers the question.*

____ 1. Where are Rifka and her family heading as she writes her letter?
  A. to Russia
  B. to Poland
  C. to prison
  D. back home

____ 2. Which family member in *Letters from Rifka* does not know about the escape?
  A. Uncle Avrum
  B. Hannah
  C. Tovah
  D. Bubbe Ruth

____ 3. How does Rifka feel about Uncle Avrum?
  A. She is angry with him.
  B. She is jealous of him.
  C. She is grateful to him.
  D. She is scornful of him.

____ 4. Which detail in *Letters from Rifka* helps you predict that guards will come to the railroad station?
  A. It is so dark that Rifka cannot see Nathan's eyes.
  B. Rifka hides her mother's candlesticks in her rucksack.
  C. At dawn, Rifka stands alone outside a boxcar.
  D. Nathan asks Rifka whether she can distract the guards.

____ 5. Which word best describes Nathan's action of returning home to warn Saul in *Letters from Rifka*?
  A. brave
  B. cowardly
  C. boastful
  D. cruel

____ 6. Why is Rifka at first happy to think that Saul will go into the army?
  A. He is cruel to her and often violent.
  B. He has always wanted to join the army.
  C. He will make the family proud.
  D. He teases her and drives her crazy.

____ 7. In *Letters from Rifka*, why does the family decide to leave their home?
   A. Family members have sent them the fare to America.
   B. They do not have enough food to survive the winter in Russia.
   C. They want to save Nathan's life and keep Saul out of the army.
   D. Their neighbors have betrayed them to the soldiers.

____ 8. Why does Rifka's mother take the candlesticks?
   A. She does not want the peasants to steal them.
   B. She hopes to use them as a weapon.
   C. They were a gift from her beloved sister.
   D. They belong to Uncle Avrum.

____ 9. What can you predict about Rifka's family from this quotation?
   They bring him back and kill him in front of his regiment as a warning to the others.
   Those who have helped him, they also die.

   A. The whole family will die.
   B. The whole family is in danger.
   C. Only Rifka's father is in danger.
   D. Only Nathan is in danger.

____ 10. In *Letters from Rifka*, what does Papa's decision to leave show about him?
   A. He hates the Russian government.
   B. He cares deeply about his family.
   C. He is desperate for money.
   D. He has given in to despair.

____ 11. In *Letters from Rifka*, why isn't Tovah allowed to hear the plans for escape?
   A. She is unable to keep a secret.
   B. She is too young to understand.
   C. The family wants to keep her from worrying.
   D. The family wants to keep her out of danger.

____ 12. Which phrase best describes Rifka's relationship with Tovah?
   A. competitive and jealous
   B. friendly but distant
   C. warm and loving
   D. cold and uncaring

## Vocabulary and Grammar

____ **13.** In which of these sentences about *Letters from Rifka* is the word *distract* used correctly?

A. Rifka's letter was written to distract Tovah's worry.

B. Papa had to distract his family to leave.

C. Rifka had to distract the guards from their search.

D. Uncle Avrum returned home to distract his daughters.

____ **14.** In *Letters from Rifka*, when the guards *emerged* from the shelter, what happened?

A. They became difficult to see.

B. They came into view.

C. They dried off.

D. They yielded to other guards.

____ **15.** In which of the following sentences about *Letters from Rifka* is the verb irregular?

A. Rifka and her family are on their way to Poland.

B. Hannah drapes a shawl over Rifka's shoulders.

C. At the train station, Papa whispers to Rifka.

D. Rifka packs Mama's candlesticks in her rucksack.

## Essay

**16.** Rifka's life is about to change completely. In an essay, describe three ways in which her life may be different. Consider what you know about Rifka's life. When does the story take place? Where has she been living? Where does Papa say they are going? Use details from *Letters from Rifka* to make your predictions.

**17.** Rifka and Nathan have character traits that will help them face the dangers and hardships of their journey. In an essay, describe those character traits. Explain how they will help Rifka and Nathan. Use details from *Letters from Rifka* to support your answer.

**18. Thinking About the Big Question: Does every Conflict have a winner?** The main conflict in *Letters From Rifka* is between Rifka's family and the government. Write an essay describing the conflict. Explain who is involved in it, and tell who the winner is.

*from* **Letters from Rifka** by Karen Hesse
"**Two Kinds**" by Amy Tan

# Integrated Language Skills: Support for Extend Your Learning

**Research and Technology:** *from* **Letters from Rifka**

Use this chart to record information for your **outline** of findings about the persecution of Jews in Russia in the early twentieth century.

| Russia in the Early Twentieth Century | Jewish Persecution in Early-Twentieth-Century Russia |
| --- | --- |
| _____ | _____ |
| _____ | _____ |
| _____ | _____ |
| _____ | _____ |
| _____ | _____ |

**Research and Technology: "Two Kinds"**

Use this chart to record information for your **outline** of findings about traditional Chinese beliefs and customs concerning the relationship between parents and children.

| Father's Role | Mother's Role | Daughter's Role | Son's Role |
| --- | --- | --- | --- |
| _____ | _____ | _____ | _____ |
| _____ | _____ | _____ | _____ |
| _____ | _____ | _____ | _____ |
| _____ | _____ | _____ | _____ |
| _____ | _____ | _____ | _____ |
| _____ | _____ | _____ | _____ |
| _____ | _____ | _____ | _____ |

## "Two Kinds" by Amy Tan
## Open-Book Test

**Short Answer** *Write your responses to the questions in this section on the lines provided.*

1. In "Two Kinds," Jing-mei's mother lost everything in China before coming to the United States. How does this experience shape her feelings about what she can expect from life in the United States? What do her expectations tell you about her character? Explain your answer with evidence from the story.

   _____

   _____

   _____

2. Early in "Two Kinds," Jing-mei imagines herself as a prodigy in many different areas. Why does she long for such fame and accomplishment?

   _____

   _____

   _____

3. In "Two Kinds," at first Jing-mei is as excited as her mother about becoming a prodigy. What changes her attitude? Use details from the story to support your answer.

   _____

   _____

   _____

4. In "Two Kinds," Auntie Lindo voices the following complaint to Jing-mei's mother:

   "All day she [Waverly] play chess. All day I have no time do nothing but dust off her winnings."

   Is she really upset about having to do all that dusting? What does this comment show about her character?

   _____

   _____

   _____

5. Read this passage from "Two Kinds." What does it help you predict about Jing-mei's future as "a Chinese Shirley Temple"? Explain how the detail leads to your prediction.

   Instead of getting big fat curls, I emerged with an uneven mass of crinkly black fuzz.

   _____

   _____

   _____

Name _____ Date _____

6. In "Two Kinds," Jing-mei and her mother argue and clash over a number of issues and incidents. Using the chart below, compare and contrast several of their key character traits.

| | Traits | | | |
|---|---|---|---|---|
| Jing-mei's mother | | | | |
| Jing-mei | | | | |

7. Jing-mei's mother has great hopes that her daughter's recital will mark her debut as a great prodigy. What details from "Two Kinds" helps you predict that things will not turn out as Jing-mei's mother planned?

_____

_____

8. In "Two Kinds," Jing-mei's refusal to continue with her piano lessons leads to an angry argument between mother and daughter. Lashing out at her mother, Jing-mei mentions her mother's dead twin daughters. Why does she mention them? Did her comment have the effect she intended? Explain your answer.

_____

_____

_____

9. Near the end of "Two Kinds," Jing-mei's mother offers to give her daughter the piano. Why does Jing-mei feel that the piano is a trophy she has won back? What does the piano represent to her?

_____

_____

_____

10. Jing-mei's mother carries great hopes for the outcome of her daughter's piano recital. Given the disastrous results, what can you tell about the meaning of the word *devastated* in the following sentence from "Two Kinds"? Explain your answer.

But my mother's expression was what devastated me: a quiet, blank look that said she had lost everything.

_____

_____

_____

**Essay**

*Write an extended response to the question of your choice or to the question or questions your teacher assigns you.*

11. In "Two Kinds," Jing-mei and her mother are alike in certain ways and different in others. Write an essay comparing and contrasting their characters. Identify and discuss at least two similarities and two differences. Support your opinion with examples from the text of "Two Kinds" to support your opinion.

12. In "Two Kinds," Jing-mei and her mother never discuss certain topics. In an essay, identify two of these topics and explain why the mother and daughter avoid these subjects. What does their avoidance tell you about their characters?

13. The title "Two Kinds" refers to the statement by the mother that there are only two kinds of daughters:

"Those who are obedient and those who follow their own mind!"

At the end of "Two Kinds," Jing-mei puts the title in a different light when she realizes that the titles "Pleading Child" and "Perfectly Contented" are "two halves of the same song." In an essay, describe the connection between these two titles and the "two kinds" of daughters. Refer to events and details in the story to support your response.

14. **Thinking About the Big Question: Does every conflict have a winner?** Consider this line from "Two Kinds":

For unlike my mother, I did not believe I could be anything I wanted to be. I could only be me.

In an essay, explain how those words describe the conflict between the daughter and her mother. Is there a winner in the conflict? Use events and details from the story to support your answer.

**Oral Response**

15. Go back to question 2, 8, or 9 or to the question your teacher assigns you. Take a few minutes to expand your answer and prepare an oral response. Find additional details in "Two Kinds" that will support your points. If necessary, make notes to guide your response.

"**Seventh Grade**" by Gary Soto
"**Melting Pot**" by Anna Quindlen
## Open-Book Test

**Short Answer** *Write your responses to the questions in this section on the lines provided.*

1. At the beginning of "Seventh Grade," Michael admits to Victor that he has been practicing a *scowl*. What does Victor think of Michael's scowl? Base your answer on the definition of *scowl*.

   _____

   _____

   _____

2. In "Seventh Grade," Victor and Michael meet on the first day of school and talk "about recent movies, baseball, their parents, and the horrors of picking grapes in order to buy their fall clothes." What do the topics of their conversation show about their lives?

   _____

   _____

   _____

3. In "Seventh Grade," Teresa asks her homeroom teacher about studying ballet. The teacher says that Mrs. Gaines "would be a good bet." What does the teacher mean by this idiom?

   _____

   _____

4. At the end of "Seventh Grade," Victor sprints to the library and borrows three French textbooks. Why does he do this?

   _____

   _____

   _____

5. The word *micro* means "small in scale." In "Melting Pot," what does Anna Quindlen mean when she says that "on a micro level most of us get along"?

   _____

   _____

6. In "Melting Pot," Anna Quindlen says that the children of the neighborhood have "sidewalk friendships." What does she mean by this idiom?

   _____

   _____

7. In "Melting Pot," Quindlen tells the reader that "about a third . . . [of her neighbors] think of squid as calamari, about a third think of it as sushi, and about a third think of it as bait." What does this observation say about the neighborhood?

_____

_____

8. Explain the literal meaning of the idioms in the chart. Then, on the line below, state whether the idioms have a similar effect on the selection or different effects. Briefly explain your position.

| Idiom | Meaning |
|---|---|
| "Seventh Grade": "He ran into his friend . . . by the water fountain." | |
| "Melting Pot": "He doesn't carry plantains." | |

_____

9. In "Melting Pot," Anna Quindlen writes, "I stood and smiled at the seedy bar." In "Seventh Grade," Victor thinks, "I'll . . . walk your dog." Which of those expressions is an idiom? Explain.

_____

_____

_____

10. Learning a new language is important to Victor in "Seventh Grade" and to the Ecuadorian family in "Melting Pot." Are Victor's reasons for wanting to learn French similar to the Ecuadorian family's reasons for wanting to learn English? Explain.

_____

_____

_____

**Essay**

*Write an extended response to the question of your choice or to the question or questions your teacher assigns you.*

11. Anna Quindlen's "melting pot" is a bustling, constantly changing neighborhood. The residents of the neighborhood come from different cultures. Would you like to live in a neighborhood like the one Quindlen describes? Why or why not? Answer this question in an essay. Use details from Quindlen's essay to support your answer.

12. In "Melting Pot," Anna Quindlen describes the cultural diversity of her neighborhood. In "Seventh Grade," Victor looks around his school and sees "brown people all around"—people like Victor. In a brief essay, write about the advantages and disadvantages of each environment: one that is culturally diverse and one that is culturally similar. Cite at least one detail from each selection to support your points.

13. Idioms are expressions that are unique to a language or a culture and cannot be understood literally. For example, the expression *strong as an ox* is an English idiom used to describe a very strong person. In your view, which story—"Seventh Grade" or "Melting Pot"—makes greater use of idioms? How do the idioms strengthen the selection? Answer these questions in an essay. Cite idioms from the selections to support your argument.

14. **Thinking About the Big Question: Does every conflict have a winner?** The main conflict in "Seventh Grade" is internal. It takes place in Victor's mind. In "Melting Pot," the conflicts are external. They take place between groups of people. In an essay, explain whether these conflicts have winners. Explain why or why not.

**Oral Response**

15. Go back to question 3, 5, or 10 or to the question your teacher assigns you. Take a few minutes to expand your answer and prepare an oral response. Find additional details in "Seventh Grade" and/or "Melting Pot" that support your points. If necessary, make notes to guide your oral response.

**"Seventh Grade"** by Gary Soto
**"Melting Pot"** by Anna Quindlen
## Selection Test A

**Critical Reading** *Identify the letter of the choice that best answers the question.*

____ 1. In "Seventh Grade," why does Victor want to take French as his elective?
   A. He loves foreign languages, and he wants to please his parents.
   B. He might travel to France one day, and a girl he likes is in the class.
   C. It is the only elective that is available by the time he gets to sign up.
   D. It is a way to avoid having to take mathematics, which he dislikes.

____ 2. In "Seventh Grade," Victor and Michael discuss "picking grapes in order to buy their fall clothes." What does this conversation reveal about their characters?
   A. They avoid working.
   B. They are hardworking.
   C. They think picking grapes is messy.
   D. They would rather gossip than work.

____ 3. In "Seventh Grade," how does Victor try to impress Teresa on the first day of French class?
   A. He scowls.
   B. He ignores her.
   C. He asks her about her summer.
   D. He pretends he speaks French.

____ 4. In "Seventh Grade," how does Victor feel about Mr. Bueller after the first French class?
   A. Victor is grateful to him.
   B. Victor is angry with him.
   C. Victor is embarrassed by him.
   D. Victor is confused about him.

____ 5. In "Melting Pot," what kind of neighborhood does the narrator live in?
   A. a suburban neighborhood
   B. an upper-class neighborhood
   C. an ethnically diverse neighborhood
   D. a warehouse district

**"The Third Wish"** by Joan Aiken
# Vocabulary Warm-up Exercises

**Exercise A** *Fill in each blank in the paragraph below with an appropriate word from Word List A. Use each word only once.*

Jackie worked [1] _____ to dock the little boat in the

[2] _____ as dark clouds moved across the sky. In a flash, a

[3] _____ wind blew up, and the boat [4] _____ at its

mooring. On [5] _____ such as this, although she was under pressure,

Jackie was carefully [6] _____ on her next move. She knew that boats

like hers were not allowed to dock at the fancy marina, but she requested permission

anyway. Fortunately, the manager [7] _____ her request. Relieved, she

did not [8] _____ another word until she was safely on shore.

**Exercise B** *Answer each question in a complete sentence. Use a word from Word List B to replace each underlined word or group of words without changing the meaning.*

**Example:** Where do the hockey players stow their <u>equipment</u>?
   *(gear) The players keep their <u>gear</u> in the locker room.*

1. How might you protect yourself in <u>severe</u> weather?

   _____

2. How might you help a friend who is <u>upset</u> about something?

   _____

3. What would you <u>most like</u> to do on a Saturday night?

   _____

4. What is a <u>faraway</u> place you have visited or would like to visit?

   _____

5. Why would it be <u>reckless</u> for someone to spend all his or her money?

   _____

6. What might be the <u>look on someone's face</u> if he or she has been kept waiting?

   _____

7. How well might someone keep his or her <u>calm</u> in an embarrassing situation?

   _____

8. What is one way of <u>expressing ideas</u> to others?

   _____

### "The Third Wish" by Joan Aiken
# Reading Warm-up A

*Read the following passage. Pay special attention to the underlined words. Then, read it again, and complete the activities. Use a separate sheet of paper for your written answers.*

"Be careful what you wish for because your wish might be <u>granted</u>." I was <u>reflecting</u> on some of my past wishes and decided that there is truth in that saying.

I used to wish for huge, truly <u>tremendous</u> things that I thought would make me happy. These were wishes I would never <u>utter</u> out loud, even to my best friend. They were too outrageous, and I knew they would never come true. There have been <u>occasions</u> when my wishes have come true, not magically, but when I made them happen. For example, I once wished I could go on a class trip to Washington, D.C. I got a summer job to pay for the trip. I had that same job, selling hot dogs to boaters on the <u>canal</u>, for the next three summers.

Then, there was my wish for a red sports car for my sixteenth birthday. The car I wished for would accelerate to 120 miles per hour in fifteen seconds. I never got that car. When I was sixteen, however, my parents helped me buy a used truck. It was gray. When the speedometer rose above 55, the body <u>thrashed</u> around like a badly loaded washing machine. Here is the thing about that truck, though: It was tough.

One day the most popular boy in school plowed his fancy wheels into a snow bank. Whom did he <u>frantically</u> call for help? You guessed it—me! That was sweet.

The money I made at my summer jobs also helped pay for my biggest wish of all, a college education. I guess that is the difference between a wish granted and a wish earned. A wish granted is a nice gift, but a wish earned keeps on giving.

1. Circle the words that tell what might be <u>granted</u>. What is a synonym for *granted*?

2. Underline the words that tell what the writer was <u>reflecting</u> on. Use *reflecting* in a sentence.

3. Circle the word that is a synonym for <u>tremendous</u>. What is the opposite of *tremendous*?

4. Underline the words that tell what the writer would never <u>utter</u> out loud. Use *utter* in a sentence.

5. On what <u>occasions</u> did the writer's wishes come true? On what other *occasions* might wishes came true?

6. Circle the word that tells who was on the <u>canal</u>. What kinds of boats might be used in a *canal*?

7. Underline the phrase that describes how the truck <u>thrashed</u> around. Use *thrashed* in a sentence.

8. Whom did the popular boy <u>frantically</u> call? Use *frantically* in a sentence.

Name _____  Date _____

*Read the following passage. Pay special attention to the underlined words. Then, read it again, and complete the activities. Use a separate sheet of paper for your written answers.*

Their names are musical: mute, trumpeter, whistling, and whooper. They can live more than 50 years in the wild. They eat mostly plants that grow in the water. They prefer to fly at night. They are known for having a serene expression as they glide calmly over the water. They are swans, birds of myth and folklore.

One of the more familiar swans is the mute swan. It is a large, all-white bird with a pinkish bill that ends in a black knob. Mute swans are not entirely silent. If you are lucky, you may hear them. They will be communicating with puppylike barking notes or loud, high-pitched purring sounds. These sounds do not travel far, so mute swans appear to be silent. This silence contributes to their supreme composure. It is as if nothing in the world could upset a mute swan. A female mute swan will become distressed, however, if another waterfowl is rash enough to invade her nesting territory. The swan will drive out the offending bird with an angry hiss and a flapping of her wings.

Swans usually mate for life, and they are good parents. The male often takes the firstborn hatchlings swimming to help out the mother while she sits on the remaining eggs. Sometimes you will see chicks riding on the back or under the wings of their parents.

Swans nest in remote Arctic islands, northern Russia, and as far south as Brazil and Australia. Many migrate to warm climates in winter. Mute swans, however, often move from frozen, freshwater habitats to nearby saltwater habitats.

Swans are one of nature's greatest beauties. To see a swan gliding peacefully on a lake is like a gift. We are instantly drawn into an island of calm far from the harsh clamor of our busy world.

1. Circle the words that tell what swans prefer to do at night. What after-school activities do you *prefer*?

2. Circle the word that tells what kind of expression swans have as they glide over water. What is a synonym for *expression*?

3. Underline the words that tell what sounds the mute swan makes when it is communicating. Use *communicating* in a sentence.

4. Underline the sentence that tells about the swan's composure. In your own words, tell what contributes to this *composure*.

5. Underline the words that tell what the swan does when it is distressed. What might a person do when he or she is *distressed*?

6. Tell what the waterfowl does that is rash. Describe a behavior you think is *rash*.

7. Underline the words that name the remote places where swans nest. Write a word that means the opposite of *remote*.

8. Circle the word that helps to define harsh. Write a sentence that describes a *harsh* sound.

**"The Third Wish"** by Joan Aiken

# Writing About the Big Question

**Does every conflict have a winner?**

## Big Question Vocabulary

| | | | |
|---|---|---|---|
| attitude | challenge | communication | competition |
| compromise | conflict | danger | desire |
| disagreement | misunderstanding | obstacle | opposition |
| outcome | resolution | struggle | understanding |

**A.** *Use one or more words from the list above to complete each sentence.*

1. We all would like to have those things that we _____ most.

2. However, a wish come true sometimes creates more _____ than joys.

3. It may even bring you into _____ with others or with your principles.

4. Your _____ toward what you want may change once you have it.

**B.** *Follow the directions in responding to each of the items below.*

1. List two examples of wishes that could have negative consequences if they came true.

   _____      _____

2. Write two to three sentences explaining how having one of the preceding wishes come true could turn out badly. Use at least two of the Big Question vocabulary words.

   _____

   _____

   _____

**C.** *Complete the sentence below. Then, write a short paragraph in which you connect this idea to the Big Question.*

   Having wishes come true can sometimes _____

   _____

   _____

   _____

   _____

   _____

Unit 2 Resources: Short Stories
**130**

## Vocabulary and Grammar

___ 13. In "The Third Wish," Mr. Peters stops himself from making a *rash* decision. Someone who makes a *rash* decision is most likely to be
A. careful.
B. selfish.
C. tired.
D. careless.

___ 14. What is the meaning of the word *malicious* as it is used in this sentence from "The Third Wish"?

He heard a harsh laugh behind him, and turning round saw the old King looking at him with a <u>malicious</u> expression.

A. happy
B. hungry
C. hateful
D. curious

___ 15. Which two words in the following sentence from "The Three Wishes" are adjectives?
Passers-by along the road heard the mournful sound of two swans.

A. along, heard
B. along, mournful
C. mournful, two
D. sound, swans

___ 16. In this sentence about "The Three Wishes," which word does the adjective *restless* modify?
She seemed restless and wandered much in the garden.

A. She
B. seemed
C. wandered
D. much

___ 17. In the following sentence from "The Three Wishes," which three words are adjectives?
There was a little man all in green with a golden crown and long beard.

A. little, all, green
B. little, golden, long
C. green, golden, beard
D. all, green, golden

## Essay

18. The King of the Forest claims that he "has yet to hear of the human being who made any good use of his three wishes." In an essay, consider whether Mr. Peters proves the old King wrong. Do Mr. Peters's wishes bring him happiness? Does he put his wishes to good use? Cite two or three events from "The Three Wishes" to support your points.

19. The characters in "The Third Wish" experience both external and internal conflicts. In an essay, define the two types of conflict, and cite an example from the story of each one. Then, describe how each conflict is resolved.

20. **Thinking About the Big Question: Does every conflict have a winner?** In an essay, explain the central conflict in "The Three Wishes" and the resolution of that conflict. Consider these questions: Who is involved in the conflict? Is the conflict internal or external? Is there a clear winner in the conflict? Who is it?

# Vocabulary Warm-up Word Lists

*Study these words from "Amigo Brothers." Then, complete the activities.*

## Word List A

**achieve** [uh CHEEV] *v.* to do something successfully after a lot of effort
Paul was proud to <u>achieve</u> his dream of becoming Player of the Year.

**barrage** [buh RAHZH] *n.* a rapid outpouring of many things at once
The Web site received a <u>barrage</u> of complaints from angry subscribers.

**fitful** [FIT fuhl] *adj.* starting and stopping in an irregular way
Loren had a <u>fitful</u> night's sleep and woke up exhausted.

**nimble** [NIM buhl] *adj.* able to move quickly and lightly
The gymnast twisted her <u>nimble</u> body into an astounding shape.

**opponent** [uh POH nuhnt] *n.* a person or team that is against you in a contest
Greta shook hands with her <u>opponent</u> after the tennis match.

**shuffle** [SHUHF uhl] *n.* a slow walk, with the feet barely leaving the ground
I recognized Vincent's tired <u>shuffle</u> as he came home from work.

**style** [STYL] *n.* the way in which something is done
Hemingway's <u>style</u> of writing is spare; he says a lot in a few words.

**surged** [SERJD] *v.* rushed forward with force
The stormy waves <u>surged</u> over the cliffs.

## Word List B

**challenger** [CHAL uhn jer] *n.* someone who competes against a champion
The <u>challenger</u> seemed ready to compete against the chess champion.

**clarity** [KLAR uh tee] *n.* clearness
Matt spoke with <u>clarity</u> about the techniques of snowboarding.

**emerging** [ee MERJ ing] *v.* coming out of somewhere
The president's motorcade was <u>emerging</u> from the tunnel.

**improvised** [IM pruh vyzd] *v.* made up something on the spot
When Sheila forgot her lines she <u>improvised</u> the words.

**mild** [MYLD] *adj.* moderate; not extreme
Bill enjoys a <u>mild</u> salsa on his tacos.

**muscular** [MUS kyoo ler] *adj.* physically strong with well-developed muscles
Jan needed a <u>muscular</u> skating partner who could lift her easily.

**numerous** [NOO mer uhs] *adj.* many
<u>Numerous</u> singers auditioned for the popular TV show.

**sparring** [SPAHR ing] *adj.* using light blows as in a practice boxing match
Rocky's <u>sparring</u> partner delivered a light punch to the jaw.

## "Amigo Brothers" by Piri Thomas
# Vocabulary Warm-up Exercises

**Exercise A** *Fill in each blank in the paragraph below with an appropriate word from Word List A. Use each word only once.*

Gladys danced around on her [1] _____ legs. She watched her

[2] _____ arrive. She noticed the girl's weary [3] _____ as she

walked slowly onto the tennis court. At first her opponent's [4] _____ was

inconsistent. Some serves were fast; some were slow. After a few [5] _____

attempts, however, the girl [6] _____ forward with a strong serve. Then, both

players sent forth a [7] _____ of hard returns. Gladys had to work hard to

[8] _____ the first win of the match.

**Exercise B** *Answer the questions with complete explanations.*

**Example:** If someone is a <u>clumsy</u> player, is he or she skillful?
*No; a clumsy player would not be skillful. He or she would trip or bump into other players.*

1. If you answer a question with <u>clarity</u>, will people understand your answer?
   _____

2. If a snake is <u>emerging</u> from a pile of leaves, is it likely you have seen its tail?
   _____

3. If you have <u>improvised</u> with a jazz band, is it likely you are a good musician?
   _____

4. If you have <u>numerous</u> things to do, do you have a great deal of free time?
   _____

5. If you are a <u>challenger</u>, are you a champion?
   _____

6. If someone is <u>muscular</u>, can he or she easily lift heavy objects?
   _____

7. If someone takes part in a <u>sparring</u> match, is he or she likely to get seriously injured?
   _____

8. If you have a <u>mild</u> manner, do you get angry often?
   _____

**"Amigo Brothers"** by Piri Thomas
# Reading Warm-up A

*Read the following passage. Pay special attention to the underlined words. Then, read it again, and complete the activities. Use a separate sheet of paper for your written answers.*

When a little guy wants to <u>achieve</u> something really, really big, he has to work hard, then harder, and harder still. Sal was a little guy who wanted to become a champion middleweight boxer. Sal was 12 years old, stood 4 feet 8 inches tall, and weighed in at about 98 pounds. He knew it would be a long, hard road for him to even get inside the ring. If he ever doubted it, his brother, who was known in boxing circles as "The Bruiser," was quick to remind him. Luckily, his brother was a sweet guy despite his crushing name.

"If you want my help, you have to stay steady on the course," his brother had said. "No <u>fitful</u> starts and stops. No 'Today I want it, tomorrow I don't.' Got that?"

"Got it! When do we start?"

"Now," his brother answered as he tossed Sal a pair of training gloves and a helmet. "Gloves up in front of your face and keep your eyes on your <u>opponent</u>. Always keep your eyes on your opponent. No matter what I do, which way I turn, never take your eyes off of me." These primary instructions were delivered as his brother moved around in a <u>nimble</u> dance. He bounced here, now there, never still, never in the same place. Sal wasn't fooled by this quick footwork. He knew his brother's <u>style</u>: tight, controlled, and fast as a viper. Suddenly his brother delivered a <u>barrage</u> of soft jabs. One, two, three, four! Sal was ready for it. He moved his gloves to block the blows, then <u>surged</u> forward with a jab to his brother's ribs.

His brother <u>shuffled</u> backward as if dancing on sand. "Good!" he exclaimed. "That's a strong beginning, Bro'. I think we've got something to work with here."

Sal grew six inches taller inside himself. He had taken his first step forward, and it was a good one.

1. Underline the words that tell what Sal wanted to <u>achieve</u>. Write about something you want to *achieve*.

2. Underline the words that mean the opposite of <u>fitful</u>. Write a sentence using the word *fitful*.

3. Circle the word that tells what you should always keep on your <u>opponent</u>. Rewrite the sentence using a synonym for *opponent*.

4. Underline the sentence that describes the brother's <u>nimble</u> dance. Give a synonym for *nimble*.

5. Underline the words that describe the brother's boxing <u>style</u>. Write about another sport that requires a similar *style*.

6. Circle the words that tell what kind of <u>barrage</u> Sal's brother delivered. Use the word *barrage* in a sentence.

7. Underline the words that tell how Sal <u>surged</u> forward. Rewrite the sentence using a synonym for *surged*.

8. Underline the words that that tell how the brother <u>shuffled</u>. Use the same meaning for the word *shuffled* in a sentence.

Unit 2 Resources: Short Stories
146

**Vocabulary and Grammar**

___ 11. When Antonio is *evading* his opponent's fists, what is he doing?
   A. He is avoiding being punched.
   B. He is fighting back with equal force.
   C. He is tricking his opponent.
   D. He is giving in to his opponent.

___ 12. Antonio's blows are *devastating*. What else might be *devastating*?
   A. a car
   B. a movie
   C. a hurricane
   D. a vacation

___ 13. Which word in this sentence from "Amigo Brothers" is an adjective?
   They fooled around with a few jabs at the air, slapped skin, and then took off.
   A. around
   B. few
   C. air
   D. slapped

___ 14. Which word in this sentence from "Amigo Brothers" does *great* modify?
   The fight had created great interest in the neighborhood.
   A. fight
   B. created
   C. interest
   D. neighborhood

**Essay**

15. In "Amigo Brothers," Antonio and Felix are best friends who fight each other in a boxing match. In an essay, describe Felix and Antonio's friendship. What do they have in common? What dreams are important to them? At the end of the match, how do they show that their friendship is important?

16. Felix and Antonio agree to act like strangers when they enter the boxing ring. They insist that despite being friends, each boxer must try his best to win the fight. Eventually, the boys determine that they should not see each other until the day of the fight. Why do you think Felix and Antonio decide to put their friendship aside while they prepare for the fight?

17. **Thinking About the Big Question: Does every conflict have a winner?** The main conflicts in "Amigo Brothers" are between the two boys and also inside each of the boys. In an essay, describe the external and internal conflicts. Do the conflicts have a clear winner? If so, who wins, and how? Use examples from the story to support your answer.

**"Amigo Brothers"** by Piri Thomas
# Selection Test B

**Critical Reading** *Identify the letter of the choice that best completes the statement or answers the question.*

_____ 1. In this passage from "Amigo Brothers," which detail shows that Felix is experiencing an internal conflict about the upcoming boxing match?

"Since we found out it was going to be me and you, I've been awake at night, pulling punches on you, trying not to hurt you."

A. He admits that he is staying awake at night thinking about the fight.
B. He states openly that the fight will be between him and Antonio.
C. He admits that he has been thinking about fighting Antonio.
D. He states that he does not want to hurt Antonio.

_____ 2. What does this passage from "Amigo Brothers" say about the conflict in the story?

"We both are *cheverote* fighters and we both want to win. But only one of us can win. There ain't no draws in the eliminations."

A. Each boy is confident that he will be the winner.
B. Each boy thinks that the other will be eliminated.
C. Both boys want to win, and they know that only one of them can win.
D. Both boys want to win, and neither wants the match to end in a draw.

_____ 3. What inference can you draw from this speech that Felix makes to Antonio in "Amigo Brothers"?

"When we get into the ring it's gotta be like we never met. We gotta be like two heavy strangers that want the same thing and only one can have it. You understand, don'tcha?"

A. Felix believes that they would be happier if they had never become friends.
B. Felix believes that after the match they will be strangers to each other.
C. Felix believes that after the match they will no longer be friends.
D. Felix believes that they must not think about their friendship during the match.

_____ 4. In "Amigo Brothers," why do Felix and Antonio agree not to see each other until after the match?
A. They are ready to fight each other.
B. They are angry with each other.
C. Each wants to focus on the match rather than on their friendship.
D. Each is afraid the other will discover something about his fighting style.

_____ 5. How are the external and internal conflicts of "Amigo Brothers" related to each other?
A. The external conflict represents each character's internal conflict.
B. The external conflict of the fight brings about an internal conflict in each character.
C. Their internal conflicts lead them to face each other, bringing about an external conflict.
D. The internal conflict is within Felix, while the external conflict is between the two friends.

____ 6. In "Amigo Brothers," how does Felix attempt to psyche himself for the big fight?
   A. Watching a fight movie, he sees himself as the champ and Antonio as the challenger.
   B. On a run by the East River, he practices his moves while envisioning Antonio's face.
   C. In the South Bronx, he fights a gang of boys who are hanging out on the street.
   D. At the gym with his trainer, he works out harder than he ever has before.

____ 7. What inference can you draw from this passage from "Amigo Brothers"?
   Antonio danced in carefully. He knew Felix had the habit of playing possum when hurt, to sucker an opponent within reach of the powerful bombs he carried in each fist.
   A. Felix can be very violent.
   B. Felix does not fight fairly.
   C. Antonio is more graceful than Felix.
   D. Antonio knows Felix's fighting style.

____ 8. What does this passage from "Amigo Brothers" suggest about Antonio's abilities as a fighter?
   Antonio danced, a joy to behold. His left hand was like a piston pumping jabs one right after another with seeming ease.
   A. He moves gracefully and punches fast.
   B. The spectators love watching him fight.
   C. He must dance better than he boxes.
   D. He punches fast but moves slowly.

____ 9. What can you infer from this passage from "Amigo Brothers"?
   They looked around and then rushed toward each other. A cry of alarm surged through Tompkins Square Park.
   A. The fighters are extremely angry with each other.
   B. The fighters have incited a riot among the spectators.
   C. The crowd is impressed with the fighters' strength and ability.
   D. The crowd thinks that the boxers are going to fight brutally.

____ 10. At the end of the boxing match, the narrator of "Amigo Brothers" says that Felix and Antonio "would always be champions to each other." What is the meaning of that statement?
   A. The boys will always think highly of each other.
   B. Both contestants have won the match.
   C. Both boys will become championship boxers.
   D. The boys are relieved that the fight is over.

____ 11. What do Antonio and Felix have in common throughout the story?
   A. Both are tall and lean.
   B. Both have a long reach.
   C. Both want to fight fairly and win.
   D. Each thinks the other is the better fighter.

## Vocabulary and Grammar

_____ 12. When a boxer is *evading* punches thrown by an opponent, he or she may be
    A. bobbing and weaving.          C. giving in.
    B. punching and jabbing.         D. playing tricks.

_____ 13. What is the meaning of the word *dispelled* in this sentence from "Amigo Brothers"?
    If Felix had any small doubt about their friendship affecting their fight, it was being
    neatly <u>dispelled</u>.

    A. increased                      C. driven away
    B. confirmed                      D. thought over

_____ 14. Something that could be described as *perpetual* is
    A. a boxing match.               C. a big storm.
    B. the ocean's tide.             D. a vacation.

_____ 15. Which two words in this sentence from "Amigo Brothers" are used as adjectives?
    In the quiet early dark, he peered over the ledge.

    A. quiet, early                  C. early, dark
    B. quiet, dark                   D. dark, ledge

_____ 16. Which word in this sentence from "Amigo Brothers" does *awesome* modify?
    Antonio's face, superimposed on the screen, was hit by the awesome blow.

    A. face                          C. hit
    B. superimposed                  D. blow

## Essay

17. At the end of "Amigo Brothers," the reader never learns which boy has earned the right to represent the Boys Club in the Golden Gloves Championship Tournament. In an essay, explain which contestant deserved to win. Support your choice with examples from the story.

18. In an essay, describe the overall external conflict and the overlapping internal conflicts in "Amigo Brothers." How does Piri Thomas weave the external and internal conflicts together to create an interesting story? Finally, describe the resolution, and tell what it teaches the characters.

19. **Thinking About the Big Question: Does every conflict have a winner?** In an essay, describe the overall external conflict and the overlapping internal conflicts in "Amigo Brothers." Do the conflicts have a clear winner? If so, who wins, and how? Use examples from the story to support your answer.

## Vocabulary and Grammar

___ 12. Which of the following sentences uses *interplanetary* correctly?

A. The interplanetary aircraft traveled from place to place on Earth.

B. The interplanetary flight from New York to London was cancelled.

C. The voyage from Earth to the moon was an interplanetary mission.

D. The interplanetary spaceship traveled from Earth to Mars.

___ 13. What does a visitor to the zoo feel if he or she is in *awe* of the horse spiders?

A. fear and wonder          C. surprise and anger

B. hostility and tenderness      D. admiration and hatred

___ 14. In the following sentence from "Zoo," which word is an adverb?

The children were always good during the month of August.

A. always            C. during

B. good             D. of

___ 15. Which word in the following sentence does the adverb *quickly* modify?

The citizens of Earth clustered around as Professor Hugo's crew quickly collected the waiting dollars.

A. around          C. collected

B. crew            D. waiting

## Essay

16. In an essay, answer these questions about the horse spiders of Kaan as they are described by Edward Hoch in "Zoo": How do the horse spiders act in their own home? How does the female act? What does the male say? What does the littlest off-spring say and do? How are the horse-spider creatures similar to human beings? How are they different from them?

17. In "Zoo," Edward Hoch is making a point about the way in which people think about those who are different from them. In an essay, explain Hoch's point more precisely. What two settings does he describe? What kinds of characters does he describe? What are some of the important things that the characters do? What does Hoch want us to learn about how people see those who are different from them?

18. **Thinking About the Big Question: Does every conflict have a winner?** In "Zoo," the people from Earth and the horse spiders from Kaan do not know very much about each other. This causes the main conflict in the story. In an essay, describe the conflict. Does the conflict have a winner? If so, who is the winner? Use details from the story to support your answer.

"**Zoo**" by Edward D. Hoch
## Selection Test B

**Critical Reading**  *Identify the letter of the choice that best completes the statement or answers the question.*

____  1. In "Zoo," for how long and when does Professor Hugo bring his zoo to the Chicago area?
A. for twenty-three days every year
B. for one day every twenty-third year
C. for a day around the twenty-third of every month
D. for six hours around the twenty-third of every August

____  2. Professor Hugo is described as wearing a "many-colored rainbow cape and top hat." What can you infer from these details of his appearance?
A. He likes colorful clothing.
B. He is a typically flashy showman.
C. He dresses up for each show.
D. He is hiding his true identity.

____  3. Professor Hugo tells his audience in Chicago, "If you enjoyed our zoo this year, telephone your friends in other cities about it." What can you infer from that remark?
A. He plans to encourage interplanetary friendships.
B. He is encouraging people to contact old friends.
C. He wants to increase his business by word of mouth.
D. He is being paid to advertise long-distance phone service.

____  4. When the horse spiders reach Kaan, they listen to Professor Hugo's "parting words" and then "scurr[y] away in a hundred different directions, seeking their homes among the rocks." What can you infer about them based on those details?
A. They respect Professor Hugo, and they live in cities among the rocks.
B. They dislike Professor Hugo, and they will never again travel with him.
C. They are tired from their long journey, and they are eager to get home.
D. They are eager to get home, and they do not all live in the same region.

____  5. From the point of view of the creatures from Kaan as they are described in "Zoo," what is strange about the people on Earth?
A. They visit zoos and speak a strange language.
B. They are horrified and fascinated by the zoo creatures.
C. They walk on two legs and wear clothing.
D. They use telephones and gather in large crowds.

____  6. In "Zoo," how do the horse spiders view the cages that separate them from visitors?
A. They believe they protect them.
B. They believe they imprison them.
C. They believe they are stage props.
D. They believe they are unnecessary.

_____ 7. In "Zoo," the he-creature remarks that the trip on the spaceship "is well worth the nineteen commocs it costs." Based on that statement, how would you define *commocs*?
A. the children of the horse-spider creatures
B. the money that is used on the planet of Kaan
C. the caves in which the horse-spider creatures dwell
D. the zoos that are constructed on the planet of Kaan

_____ 8. The behavior of the humans and the horse spiders in "Zoo" suggests the story is
A. about people's differences and similarities.
B. about people's differences in intelligence.
C. about people's curiosity about nature.
D. about people's curiosity about space travel.

_____ 9. At the end of "Zoo," we learn that horse spiders pay Professor Hugo to take them on voyages. From that information, the reader may infer that Professor Hugo
A. is making a mistake.
B. is a clever showman.
C. is interested in scientific research.
D. is an extremely wealthy man.

_____ 10. In "Zoo," Edward Hoch takes a look at people's views of those who are different from them. What is his theme?
A. People want to meet those who are different from them so they can learn from them.
B. People want to meet those who are different from them because they are curious.
C. People fear those who are different from them and so fail to see how they are similar.
D. People shy away from people who are different from them and so fail to learn from them.

_____ 11. Which of the following details best supports the theme of "Zoo"?
A. The people of Chicago crowd around as Professor Hugo's crew collects their money.
B. The people of Chicago are both horrified and fascinated by the horse-spider creatures.
C. The creatures of Kaan listen to the professor's parting words and then scurry away.
D. The young horse spider runs up the wall of its cave before speaking of its adventure.

**Vocabulary and Grammar**

_____ 12. Which of the following scenes from "Zoo" shows characters in *awe*?
A. Crowds come to the zoo and willingly pay to see the horse-spider creatures.
B. Professor Hugo greets the crowd wearing a colorful cape and a top hat.
C. The crowds are both horrified and fascinated by the horse spiders.
D. The horse spiders leave their cages and scurry away to their homes.

____ **13.** The fact that Hugo's zoo is *interplanetary* means that it travels
   A. from one planet to another.
   B. from place to place on one planet.
   C. with creatures from another planet.
   D. from city to city on one continent.

____ **14.** In the following sentence from "Zoo," which word does the adverb *slowly* modify?
      And the crowds slowly filed by.
   A. And
   B. crowds
   C. filed
   D. by

____ **15.** Which word in the following sentence from "Zoo" is an adverb?
      "We must go now, but we will return next year on this date."
   A. must
   B. now
   C. next
   D. date

**Essay**

16. In an essay, discuss the theme of "Zoo." Consider these questions: What are the settings, and how do they help you determine the theme? What do characters say and do that helps you discover the theme? Mention at least three details in the story to support your points.

17. In an essay, describe Professor Hugo and the way in which he makes money. What does he look like? What does he say to his audience? Why do people pay him? Does he take advantage of people to make money? Cite at least two examples from "Zoo" to support your points.

18. **Thinking About the Big Question: Does every conflict have a winner?** In "Zoo," what are the main forms of conflict between the people from Earth and the horse spiders from Kaan? Does the conflict have a winner? If so, who is the winner? Use details from the story to support your answer.

12. In an essay, explain how "Ribbons" illustrates the idea that differences between cultures can lead to misunderstandings and conflict. Consider these questions in an essay: What are the main cultural differences portrayed in the story? How does Stacy react to her grandmother? How do Stacy and her grandmother resolve their differences? What lessons about cultural differences does the story hold for readers? Use examples from the story to support your points.

13. In "Ribbons," whom do you think is more to blame for the conflict that develops between Stacy and Grandmother? Or are they both equally responsible? Express your opinion in an essay supported by clear reasoning and specific examples from the story.

14. **Thinking About the Big Question: Does every conflict have a winner?** In "Ribbons," Stacy and her grandmother have trouble getting along. In an essay, describe their conflict. Consider how Grandmother treats Stacy in the beginning and how their feelings have changed by the end. Explain whether their conflict has a clear winner and, if it does, who the winner is.

## Oral Response

15. Go back to question 2, 5, or 9 or to the question your teacher assigns to you. Take a few minutes to expand your answer and prepare an oral response. Find additional details in "Ribbons" that will support your points. If necessary, make notes to guide your response.

**"Ribbons"** by Laurence Yep
# Selection Test A

**Critical Reading** *Identify the letter of the choice that best answers the question.*

_____ 1. In "Ribbons," from where has Grandmother just arrived?
   A. China
   B. San Francisco
   C. Hong Kong
   D. Los Angeles

_____ 2. Why does Grandmother get out of the car before Stacy's father can help her?
   A. She does not like Stacy's father.
   B. She wants to get out by herself.
   C. She is too shy to accept his help.
   D. She is eager to greet her daughter.

_____ 3. In "Ribbons," Ian is relieved when he realizes that Grandmother speaks English. What inference can the reader draw from this detail?
   A. He does not speak Chinese.
   B. He does not want to talk to her.
   C. He wants her to teach him Chinese.
   D. He does not want Stacy to talk to her.

_____ 4. In "Ribbons," Grandmother reacts to Stacy's hug by stiffening and snapping at her. What inference can the reader draw from this detail?
   A. She is not used to people showing affection.
   B. She is afraid Stacy will cause her to fall over.
   C. She does not want Stacy to get her dirty.
   D. She thinks that hugs can spread disease.

_____ 5. In "Ribbons," what does Stacy ask her father once her grandmother has arrived?
   A. She asks to have her own room back again.
   B. She asks to attend ballet class again.
   C. She asks to share her room with Grandmother.
   D. She asks to read fairy tales to Ian.

_____ 6. In "Ribbons," why does Grandmother spoil Ian?
   A. He is young.
   B. He is cute.
   C. He is smart.
   D. He is a boy.

____ 7. What does Stacy discover when she puts on her satin toe shoe?

    A. The shoe is too small.

    B. The ribbons are too long.

    C. The ribbons have come off.

    D. The shoe has fallen apart.

____ 8. In "Ribbons," why does Grandmother get angry when she sees the ribbons of Stacy's toe shoe?

    A. She thinks they are too grown-up for Stacy.

    B. She thinks Stacy will hurt her with them.

    C. She thinks they are hurting Stacy's feet.

    D. She thinks Stacy likes ballet too much.

____ 9. In "Ribbons," why is Grandmother ashamed of her feet?

    A. They were bound when she was a child and are now misshapen.

    B. They were hurt in a childhood accident and are badly scarred.

    C. They were misshapen at birth and made fun of by her parents.

    D. They are not as beautiful as the feet of other Chinese women.

____ 10. How does Stacy treat her grandmother once she learns about her grandmother's feet?

    A. She flatters her.

    B. She helps her get around.

    C. She makes fun of her.

    D. She stops ignoring her.

____ 11. Why is "The Little Mermaid" important to the theme of "Ribbons"?

    A. It is a story that Grandmother is familiar with from her childhood in China.

    B. It allows Stacy and Grandmother to talk about Grandmother's bound feet.

    C. It causes Grandmother and Ian to argue about the meaning of the story.

    D. It helps Grandmother feel comfortable about letting Stacy see her feet.

____ 12. What does the title of "Ribbons" refer to?

    A. both the ribbons that bound Grandmother's feet and the ribbons on Stacy's toe shoes

    B. both the ribbons that bound Grandmother's feet and the ribbons worn by the mermaid

    C. only the ribbons on Stacy's toe shoes

    D. only the ribbons worn by the mermaid

## Vocabulary and Grammar

____ 13. In "Ribbons," what does it mean when Stacy's father's face becomes red from the *exertion* of carrying Grandmother's belongings?

    **A.** He is hot.

    **B.** He is working hard.

    **C.** He is too busy to wash his face.

    **D.** He is angry because no one is helping him.

____ 14. In "Ribbons," what does the writer mean when he says that Grandmother tries "to *coax* a smile from Ian"?

    **A.** She is forcing him to smile.

    **B.** She really wants him to smile.

    **C.** She is funny, and he wants to smile.

    **D.** She is gently trying to make him smile.

____ 15. Which word in the following sentence from "Ribbons" is an adverb?

    Though she was stiff at first, she gradually softened in my arms.

    **A.** she

    **B.** stiff

    **C.** gradually

    **D.** softened

## Essay

16. In "Ribbons," Stacy and her grandmother have trouble getting along. In an essay, describe their conflict, and explain how Stacy and Grandmother are able to grow closer at the end of the story. Consider these questions: How does Grandmother treat Stacy in the beginning of the story? What angers her about Stacy's toe shoes? What does Stacy learn about her grandmother's feet? How does the story of the little mermaid help them resolve their conflict?

17. The theme of a story is its central message or insight. In "Ribbons," the theme is that cultural differences can be bridged through communication. In an essay, discuss how Laurence Yep reveals this theme. Answer these questions: What objects in the story are important to the theme? How does the title "Ribbons" relate to the theme? How do the main characters' actions support the theme?

18. **Thinking About the Big Question: Does every conflict have a winner?** In "Ribbons," Stacy and her grandmother have trouble getting along. In an essay, describe their conflict. Consider how Grandmother treats Stacy in the beginning and how their feelings have changed by the end. Does their conflict have a clear winner? If so, who is it?

**"After Twenty Years"** by O. Henry
**"He—y, Come On O—ut!"** by Shinichi Hoshi
# Selection Test A

**Critical Reading** *Identify the letter of the choice that best answers the question.*

____ 1. In "After Twenty Years," what has happened to the restaurant where the two friends had agreed to meet?

    **A.** It has closed for the evening.

    **B.** It has changed management.

    **C.** It has forbidden the man to enter.

    **D.** It has been closed for five years.

____ 2. In "After Twenty Years," why does the policeman make a point of asking the man in the doorway whether he plans to wait for Jimmy Wells to show up?

    **A.** He is testing him to find out whether he is a trusted friend.

    **B.** He wants to see whether he has time to call another officer to arrest him.

    **C.** He needs time to change out of his uniform and come back to surprise his friend.

    **D.** He needs time to find out whether there is an outstanding warrant for his arrest.

____ 3. Which of the following statements best summarizes the meaning of this quotation from "After Twenty Years"?

    *"It [twenty years] sometimes changes a good man into a bad one."*

    **A.** A life of crime can change a good man into a bad man.

    **B.** The West is likely to change a good man into a bad man.

    **C.** Over the course of twenty years, a good man may turn to crime.

    **D.** You are lucky that life in the West did not change you into a bad man.

____ 4. What is ironic about Jimmy and "Silky" Bob in "After Twenty Years"?

    **A.** One has become a police officer, and one has become a criminal.

    **B.** One has grown taller, while the other has grown shorter with age.

    **C.** Both of them have become criminals.

    **D.** Neither of them ever liked the other.

____ 5. In "He—y, Come On O—ut!" how do the villagers come to discover the hole?

    **A.** A landslide has swept away a shrine that had covered it.

    **B.** A typhoon has destroyed a building that had covered it.

    **C.** A child from the village falls into it.

    **D.** A construction worker notices it.

___ 6. In "He—y, Come On O—ut!" how does the scientist who comes to examine the hole behave?

  A. He acts as if the hole will go away on its own.

  B. He acts as if the hole is an unnatural event.

  C. He acts as if the hole is not at all unusual.

  D. He acts as if he has seen many such holes.

___ 7. In "He—y, Come On O—ut!" who offers to fill the hole?

  A. a newspaper reporter                    C. a government worker
  B. one of the scientists                   D. one of the concessionaires

___ 8. What is ironic about the ending of "He—y, Come On O—ut!"?

  A. The hole is filled and eventually pollutes the entire village.

  B. The city keeps expanding until the village is swallowed up.

  C. A voice shouts from the sky and a pebble falls toward the city.

  D. The hole never fills up, and the city becomes cleaner and better.

___ 9. Which of the following choices is an example of dramatic irony?

  A. An audience can predict that the hero of a story will die.

  B. A character says, "That dress looks so good on you," while thinking that it looks awful.

  C. Readers know who the villain is, but the other characters do not realize it.

  D. A politician who criticizes his opponent's moral character is convicted of lying under oath.

___ 10. Which of the following choices is an example of situational irony?

  A. A girl who was always in trouble grows up to become a police officer.

  B. Unexpected guests arrive, the house is a mess, and the host says, "I'm glad you came."

  C. Readers know that one character in a story will die, but none of the characters know it.

  D. Readers realize that a plot is based on the plot of a much older story that ends tragically.

___ 11. Which word best describes the endings of "After Twenty Years" and "He—y, Come On O—ut!"?

  A. sad                                     C. tragic
  B. surprising                              D. funny

___ 12. Which part of "He—y, Come On O—ut!" makes it less realistic than "After Twenty Years"?

  A. a deep hole that never fills up         C. constructions workers taking
  B. people burying nuclear waste               breaks
                                             D. villagers moving a sacred shrine

## Vocabulary

___ **13.** When "Silky" Bob says that "each of us ought to have our *destiny* worked out," what does he mean?

    **A.** Their futures will have been decided.

    **B.** They will have solved their puzzles.

    **C.** They will have paid off their debts.

    **D.** Their unhappiness will have eased.

___ **14.** Which of the following choices describes a *plausible* explanation?

    **A.** one that everyone has rejected

    **B.** one that makes everyone happy

    **C.** one that is scientific

    **D.** one that makes sense

___ **15.** Who would be most likely to make a *proposal*?

    **A.** an architect who hopes to design a building

    **B.** a nurse who is caring for a sick patient

    **C.** a student who has finished her homework

    **D.** a construction worker who is on a break

## Essay

**16.** Both "After Twenty Years" and "He—y, Come On O—ut!" contain irony. In an essay, discuss the use of irony in these stories. For each story, identify the irony as situational, verbal, or dramatic. Then, explain why you have identified it that way. Cite details in each story that support your choice.

**17.** Stories that make use of irony often have surprise endings. In an essay, compare the endings of "After Twenty Years" and "He—y, Come On O—ut!" Consider these questions: What is surprising about each ending? Which ending is more surprising? What makes it more surprising? Why is the other story less surprising—does something tip you off to the ending? If so, what is it?

**18.** **Thinking About the Big Question: Does every conflict have a winner?** Both "After Twenty Years" and "He—y, Come On O—ut" center on conflicts. Think about the conflict between Bob and the policeman in "After Twenty Years" and between the concessionaire and the villagers in "He—y, Come On O—ut!" Then, in an essay, describe each conflict. Explain whether you think that each conflict has a clear winner. Use details from the stories to support your answer.

**"After Twenty Years"** by O. Henry
**"He—y, Come On O—ut!"** by Shinichi Hoshi
## Selection Test B

**Critical Reading** *Identify the letter of the choice that best completes the statement or answers the question.*

____ 1. Why does the policeman in "After Twenty Years" slow down when he sees the man in the doorway?
A. He is lonely and welcomes the chance to talk to someone.
B. He immediately recognizes the man in the doorway.
C. He is generally suspicious of people standing in doorways.
D. He is keeping the appointment to meet his friend.

____ 2. In "After Twenty Years," the fact that the man in the doorway provides the police officer with a long explanation shows that
A. he is unfamiliar with the neighborhood.
B. he does not recognize his old friend.
C. he has something to hide.
D. he is guilty of a crime.

____ 3. In "After Twenty Years," why does "Silky" Bob fail to recognize his old friend?
A. Jimmy had always said that he had no respect for policemen.
B. Jimmy was unattractive as a young man.
C. Bob cannot imagine that Jimmy would become a policeman.
D. Bob does not expect Jimmy to show up.

____ 4. In "After Twenty Years," when the man claiming to be Jimmy first approaches "Silky" Bob, what *first* arouses Bob's suspicions about him?
A. his height                  C. his walk
B. his nose                    D. his voice

____ 5. At what point in "After Twenty Years" does Jimmy first realize that his friend is a wanted criminal?
A. when he sees Bob's large diamond scarfpin
B. when Bob strikes a match that lights up his face
C. as soon as Jimmy walks up to the doorway
D. minutes after Jimmy walks away from Bob

____ 6. What is ironic about the ending of "After Twenty Years"?
A. Jimmy is the policeman who talks to Bob and then has Bob arrested.
B. The man who shows up claiming to be Jimmy is really a criminal.
C. Bob is sure that Jimmy is alive and that he will keep the appointment.
D. Jimmy arrests Bob when he realizes that he is a wanted criminal.

____ 7. In "He—y, Come On O—ut!" what is remarkable about the hole found under the shrine?
A. It is in a holy place.                  C. It seems to be bottomless.
B. It is very wide.                        D. It is filled with different things.

15. Many objects circle the sun, including _____ .
    A. raindrops
    B. snowflakes
    C. asteroids
    D. atmospheric

16. The pipes differed greatly and were of _____ lengths.
    A. averaging
    B. varying
    C. contrary
    D. paralyzing

17. This snake is the type that releases _____ when it bites.
    A. venom
    B. symptoms
    C. punctures
    D. nausea

18. Cats and tigers live in different _____ .
    A. cultural
    B. organizations
    C. environments
    D. communal

19. The neighborhood cleanup after the storm was organized by the local _____ .
    A. citizenry
    B. lawmakers
    C. schoolteachers
    D. varmints

20. Strangely, these two important events occurred _____ .
    A. dutifully
    B. leisurely
    C. distinctively
    D. simultaneously

# Diagnostic Tests and Vocabulary in Context
## Use and Interpretation

The Diagnostic Tests and Vocabulary in Context were developed to assist teachers in making the most appropriate assignment of *Prentice Hall Literature* program selections to students. The purpose of these assessments is to indicate the degree of difficulty that students are likely to have in reading/comprehending the selections presented in the *following* unit of instruction. Tests are provided at six separate times in each grade level—a *Diagnostic Test* (to be used prior to beginning the year's instruction) and a *Vocabulary in Context,* the final segment of the Benchmark Test, appearing at the end of each of the first five units of instruction. Note that the tests are intended for use not as summative assessments for the prior unit, but as guidance for assigning literature selections in the upcoming unit of instruction.

The structure of all Diagnostic Tests and Vocabulary in Context in this series is the same. All test items are four-option, multiple-choice items. The format is established to assess a student's ability to construct sufficient meaning from the context sentence to choose the only provided word that fits both the semantics (meaning) and syntax (structure) of the context sentence. All words in the context sentences are chosen to be "below-level" words that students reading at this grade level should know. All answer choices fit *either* the meaning or structure of the context sentence, but only the correct choice fits *both* semantics and syntax. All answer choices—both correct answers and incorrect options—are key words chosen from specifically taught words that will occur in the subsequent unit of program instruction. This careful restriction of the assessed words permits a sound diagnosis of students' current reading achievement and prediction of the most appropriate level of readings to assign in the upcoming unit of instruction.

The assessment of vocabulary in context skill has consistently been shown in reading research studies to correlate very highly with "reading comprehension." This is not surprising as the format essentially assesses comprehension, albeit in sentence-length "chunks." Decades of research demonstrate that vocabulary assessment provides a strong, reliable prediction of comprehension achievement—the purpose of these tests. Further, because this format demands very little testing time, these diagnoses can be made efficiently, permitting teachers to move forward with critical instructional tasks rather than devoting excessive time to assessment.

It is important to stress that while the Diagnostic and Vocabulary in Context were carefully developed and will yield sound assignment decisions, they were designed to *reinforce*, not supplant, teacher judgment as to the most appropriate instructional placement for individual students. Teacher judgment should always prevail in making placement—or indeed other important instructional—decisions concerning students.

# Diagnostic Tests and Vocabulary in Context
# Branching Suggestions

These tests are designed to provide maximum flexibility for teachers. Your *Unit Resources* books contain the 40-question **Diagnostic Test** and 20-question **Vocabulary in Context** tests. At *PHLitOnline*, you can access the Diagnostic Test and complete 40-question Vocabulary in Context tests. Procedures for administering the tests are described below. Choose the procedure based on the time you wish to devote to the activity and your comfort with the assignment decisions relative to the individual students. Remember that your judgment of a student's reading level should always take precedence over the results of a single written test.

Feel free to use different procedures at different times of the year. For example, for early units, you may wish to be more confident in the assignments you make—thus, using the "two-stage" process below. Later, you may choose the quicker diagnosis, confirming the results with your observations of the students' performance built up throughout the year.

The **Diagnostic Test** is composed of a single 40-item assessment. Based on the results of this assessment, make the following assignment of students to the reading selections in Unit 1:

| Diagnostic Test Score | Selection to Use |
|---|---|
| If the student's score is 0–25 | more accessible |
| If the student's score is 26–40 | more challenging |

Outlined below are the three basic options for administering **Vocabulary in Context** and basing selection assignments on the results of these assessments.

1. For a one-stage, quicker diagnosis using the *20-item* test in the *Unit Resources:*

| Vocabulary in Context Test Score | Selection to Use |
|---|---|
| If the student's score is 0–13 | more accessible |
| If the student's score is 14–20 | more challenging |

2. If you wish to confirm your assignment decisions with a *two-stage* diagnosis:

| Stage 1: Administer the 20-item test in the *Unit Resources* | |
|---|---|
| Vocabulary in Context Test Score | Selection to Use |
| If the student's score is 0–9 | more accessible |
| If the student's score is 10–15 | (Go to Stage 2.) |
| If the student's score is 16–20 | more challenging |

| Stage 2: Administer items 21–40 from *PHLitOnline* | |
|---|---|
| Vocabulary in Context Test Score | Selection to Use |
| If the student's score is 0–12 | more accessible |
| If the student's score is 13–20 | more challenging |

3. If you base your assignment decisions on the full 40-item **Vocabulary in Context** from *PHLitOnline:*

| Vocabulary in Context Test Score | Selection to Use |
|---|---|
| If the student's score is 0–25 | more accessible |
| If the student's score is 26–40 | more challenging |

8. <u>sending members of the family away before they could</u> <u>be captured;</u> *Precaution* means "something done ahead of time to keep away danger."

## Writing About the Big Question, p. 66

**A. Sample Answer**

may be forced; homes; country; they care about

**B. Sample Answers**

1. Native Americans; Jews
2. Battles with the U.S. government forced many Native Americans to flee their homelands. They struggled to adapt to reservations that often did not have the resources and climates that they were used to. They sometimes battled the government over how to raise their own children.

**C. Sample Answer**

The true losers in a war are the children who lose their loved ones, their homes, or their countries—or all of the above. They lose everything they have ever known and have to start over someplace new. Their lives can become very difficult. Even if their side eventually "wins" the war, they themselves still lose in many ways.

### *from* Letters from Rifka by Karen Hesse

## Reading: Read Ahead to Verify Predictions and Reread to Look for Details, p. 67

For incorrect predictions, **Event and Detail** follow **Verification:**

2. Incorrect / Rifka never reveals just what happens between her and the guards, but readers can tell from the first line of the selection ("We made it!") that she somehow succeeded.
3. Correct
4. Incorrect / They leave without the papers. Papa says, "There is no time for papers."

## Literary Analysis: Characters, p. 68

**A.** Sample Answers

1. brave, thoughtful, caring
2. decisive, careful, loving

**B.** 1. C; 2. A; 3. E; 4. B; 5. D

## Vocabulary Builder, p. 69

**A.** Sample Answers

1. She might have made up a story about what she was doing on the train.
2. Most likely, he would have been arrested by the guards.
3. They were gathered close together to hide from the soldiers who were coming in search of Nathan.
4. He might not have supported the cause he and his fellow soldiers were fighting for.

5. Peasants are often uneducated and poor, so they would see it as an opportunity to enrich themselves.
6. It was necessary to protect Tovah from soldiers who might question her.

**B.** Sample Answers

1. When you retract a statement, you take it back.
2. If both sides call numerous witnesses, the trial could go on for a long time.
3. They might groom themselves carefully and wear nice clothes.

## Enrichment: Aleksandr Pushkin, p. 70

**Sample Answers**

1. The speaker might mean lands to which Russians immigrate.
2. The speaker might be referring to the Russian people who are trapped by "age-old rites," old beliefs and customs.
3. Rifka is like the bird set free in that she has fled old Russia and its "age-old rites" to find a new home and a new life where she will be freer.

## Open-Book Test, p. 71

**Short Answer**

1. Rifka likes Nathan much better—she shows concern for his safety and well-being throughout the story. On the other hand, she wishes that Saul, her other brother, would disappear, and she shows no concern or fondness for him.

   **Difficulty:** *Easy*   **Objective:** *Literary Analysis*

2. Rifka is ashamed at wanting to see her brother Saul taken away by the police because she soon realizes that his situation shows that the whole family is in danger. Her shame shows that, although she is capable of petty dislikes, she is also mature and wise enough to understand that the threat to her family is more important than her private feelings about her brother.

   **Difficulty:** *Challenging*   **Objective:** *Literary Analysis*

3. If Nathan is facing special punishment for being Jewish, then there must be widespread prejudice against Jews at this time in Russia. Rifka's family is fleeing to America to escape from this prejudice against their people.

   **Difficulty:** *Easy*   **Objective:** *Interpretation*

4. Students may predict Rifka is so protective toward Nathan that she goes as far as giving herself up to the guards to distract them from Nathan. It is not possible to verify this prediction from details in the story.

   **Difficulty:** *Average*   **Objective:** *Reading*

5. Some students might note that for Mama, the candlesticks represent a positive aspect of their traditional way of life that she would like to keep with her on their journey to a new land. Others might think that the candlesticks are something of value that the family might sell in a moment of need on their journey.

   **Difficulty:** *Challenging*   **Objective:** *Interpretation*

6. The guards will soon notice Rifka. The phrase "at first" hints at this.
   **Difficulty:** *Easy*   **Objective:** *Reading*
7. Students might note that Rifka is an emotional person who values her friends and relatives and does not want to leave them without a chance to say goodbye. They might also note that she is an adventurous person who is proud that the family is going to America and wishes she could share this news with others.
   **Difficulty:** *Average*   **Objective:** *Literary Analysis*
8. Noting how highly Rifka values her book (which is actually a book of poetry, although few students will know this), students might predict the following careers for Rifka: teacher, because she loves knowledge and writing; writer, because she admires the work of other writers; librarian, because she values and cares about books. Students should write "no" under the "Predictions Verified by Text" column, since the excerpt does not tell about Rifka's adulthood.
   **Difficulty:** *Average*   **Objective:** *Reading*
9. Rifka's letter-writing allows the girls to remain close, even from a long distance; the letters also give Rifka a way to sort out her thoughts and feelings during this difficult time of danger and transition in her life.
   **Difficulty:** *Challenging*   **Objective:** *Interpretation*
10. came into view
    **Difficulty:** *Average*   **Objective:** *Vocabulary*

## Essay

11. Students might note that when the family arrives in America, Rifka will have to learn a new language and new customs. She will probably go to school, make new friends, and be reunited with brothers she has not seen in a long time. She and her family might have greater opportunities for a better life in America, where there is less prejudice against Jews than there was in Russia at that time.
    **Difficulty:** *Easy*   **Objective:** *Essay*
12. Students will likely note that both Nathan and Rifka demonstrate courage. Their courage will help them face other dangers on the journey. Both also care deeply about the family, which may help other family members endure the trip. Students may also comment on Rifka's ability to adapt to change, a trait that will help her handle the uncertainties of the future. Both characters also seem honest, trustworthy, and intelligent. Rifka keeps the family's plans a secret before they leave, and Nathan is clever enough to escape from the Russian army.
    **Difficulty:** *Average*   **Objective:** *Essay*
13. The main condition in Russia that causes Rifka's family to leave is prejudice against Jews—this is evident from the especially harsh punishment given to Jewish deserters from the army. It is also evident that Russia is a poor country with limited opportunities for everyone, especially Jews. By leaving, the family will lose their traditional way of life, their friends, and some of their relatives. In their new country, the family will have to deal with strange customs and learn a new language, but with less prejudice against Jews and better economic conditions, they will probably have a better chance to live a comfortable, fulfilling life.
    **Difficulty:** *Challenging*   **Objective:** *Essay*
14. Students will probably note that the main conflict is between Rifka's family and the government, which is dominated by prejudice against Jews, treats them more harshly than other groups, and limits their opportunities. Rifka's family won when they escaped to America. Students may point out that if the government had won, the whole family might have died. Other students might argue that prejudice is a no-win situation: the people who practice it become like beasts, and the people who try to escape from it have their lives uprooted.
    **Difficulty:** *Average*   **Objective:** *Essay*

## Oral Response

15. Students should give oral explanations in response to the questions they choose or that are assigned to them.
    **Difficulty:** *Average*   **Objective:** *Oral Interpretation*

## Selection Test A, p. 74
### Critical Reading

| | | |
|---|---|---|
| 1. ANS: B | DIF: Easy | OBJ: Comprehension |
| 2. ANS: D | DIF: Easy | OBJ: Comprehension |
| 3. ANS: C | DIF: Easy | OBJ: Interpretation |
| 4. ANS: D | DIF: Easy | OBJ: Reading Skill |
| 5. ANS: A | DIF: Easy | OBJ: Literary Analysis |
| 6. ANS: D | DIF: Easy | OBJ: Literary Analysis |
| 7. ANS: C | DIF: Easy | OBJ: Interpretation |
| 8. ANS: A | DIF: Easy | OBJ: Comprehension |
| 9. ANS: B | DIF: Easy | OBJ: Reading Skill |
| 10. ANS: B | DIF: Easy | OBJ: Literary Analysis |
| 11. ANS: D | DIF: Easy | OBJ: Comprehension |
| 12. ANS: C | DIF: Easy | OBJ: Interpretation |

### Vocabulary and Grammar

| | | |
|---|---|---|
| 13. ANS: C | DIF: Easy | OBJ: Vocabulary |
| 14. ANS: B | DIF: Easy | OBJ: Vocabulary |
| 15. ANS: A | DIF: Easy | OBJ: Grammar |

### Essay

16. Students might note that Rifka's family is likely to encounter dangers and will certainly be uncomfortable on their journey. Assuming they arrive safely in America, Rifka will have to learn a new language and new customs. She will most likely attend school. She will

miss her relatives and old friends, and she will have to make new friends. She will be reunited with brothers she has probably not seen in a long time, and she will have to get to know them again.

**Difficulty:** *Easy*

**Objective:** *Essay*

17. Students will likely note that both Nathan and Rifka demonstrate courage, Nathan when he deserts the army to warn Saul that he will soon be forced to join and Rifka when she declares that she will be able to distract the guards. That courage will help them face other dangers on the journey. Both also care deeply about their family, as Nathan's desertion and Rifka's remarks about her family members show—she is grateful to Avrum, loves her grandmother, treasures a gift given her by Tovah. Students might point out that their bravery and commitment to the family may motivate the less courageous family members.

**Difficulty:** *Easy*

**Objective:** *Essay*

18. Students should describe the conflict as between Rifka's family and the government, which is prejudiced against Jews. It treats them more harshly than other groups and limits their opportunities. Rifka's family won the conflict when they escaped to America.

**Difficulty:** *Easy*

**Objective:** *Essay*

## Selection Test B, p. 77

### Critical Reading

| | | |
|---|---|---|
| 1. ANS: B | DIF: Average | OBJ: Interpretation |
| 2. ANS: A | DIF: Challenging | OBJ: Interpretation |
| 3. ANS: C | DIF: Challenging | OBJ: Interpretation |
| 4. ANS: D | DIF: Average | OBJ: Reading Skill |
| 5. ANS: B | DIF: Average | OBJ: Reading Skill |
| 6. ANS: B | DIF: Challenging | OBJ: Reading Skill |
| 7. ANS: C | DIF: Average | OBJ: Comprehension |
| 8. ANS: D | DIF: Average | OBJ: Literary Analysis |
| 9. ANS: A | DIF: Average | OBJ: Reading Skill |
| 10. ANS: B | DIF: Challenging | OBJ: Literary Analysis |
| 11. ANS: A | DIF: Challenging | OBJ: Interpretation |
| 12. ANS: C | DIF: Challenging | OBJ: Literary Analysis |
| 13. ANS: A | DIF: Average | OBJ: Comprehension |
| 14. ANS: C | DIF: Average | OBJ: Interpretation |

### Vocabulary and Grammar

| | | |
|---|---|---|
| 15. ANS: C | DIF: Average | OBJ: Vocabulary |
| 16. ANS: A | DIF: Average | OBJ: Vocabulary |
| 17. ANS: D | DIF: Average | OBJ: Grammar |
| 18. ANS: C | DIF: Average | OBJ: Grammar |
| 19. ANS: B | DIF: Challenging | OBJ: Grammar |

### Essay

20. Students will likely note that both Nathan and Rifka demonstrate courage, Nathan when he deserts to warn his brother and Rifka when she declares that she will be able to distract the guards. Their courage will help them face other dangers on the journey. Both also care deeply about their family, as Nathan's desertion and Rifka's remarks about her family members show—she is grateful to Avrum, loves her grandmother, treasures a gift given her by Tovah. Students might point out that their bravery and commitment to the family may motivate the less courageous family members. Students may also comment on Rifka's ability to adapt to change, a trait that will probably help her deal with the uncertainties of the future.

**Difficulty:** *Average*

**Objective:** *Essay*

21. Students might note that Rifka is clearly extremely fond of Nathan (when she sees him at the door, joy fills her heart), so she probably wants to win his admiration. She may also wish to prove that Saul is wrong about her—she is not too small to be noticed. Finally, she knows the extreme danger her family faces. Their safety depends on her efforts, and because she loves them deeply, she will act to make sure they escape safely. Her courage and imagination are traits that may help her succeed.

**Difficulty:** *Challenging*

**Objective:** *Essay*

22. Students will probably note that the main conflict is between Rifka's family and the government, which is dominated by prejudice against Jews, treats them more harshly than other groups, and limits their opportunities. Rifka's family won when they escaped to America. Students may point out that if the government had won, the whole family might have died. Other students might argue that prejudice is a no-win situation: the people who practice it become like beasts, and the people who try to escape from it have their lives uprooted.

**Difficulty:** *Average*

**Objective:** *Essay*

## "Two Kinds" by Amy Tan

### Vocabulary Warm-up Exercises, p. 81

**A.** 1. sulky
2. uneven
3. nervousness
4. regret
5. arched
6. talented
7. exist
8. assured

**B.** Sample Answers
1. F; *Images* are mental pictures, and most artists do have mental pictures of what they plan to paint.

2. T; *Heaving* means "moving up and down," and when you breathe heavily, your chest rises and falls, or heaves.

3. F; An *assortment* is a collection or a variety, so if there is a large assortment, there are many choices.

4. T; *Fascinated* means "very interested by something," so its opposite would be *bored*, which means "uninterested in anything."

5. F; *Miniature* means "very small," so an adult would not fit comfortably in a miniature chair.

6. F; *Throughout* means "from start to finish," so if you leave early, you will not have stayed for the whole performance.

7. T; *Purely* means "entirely," so something that happens purely by design was planned.

8. F; *Petals* are the colorful parts of flowers that are shaped like leaves; all flowers have petals.

## Reading Warm-up A, p. 82

Words that students are to circle appear in parentheses.

**Sample Answers**

1. the results of their efforts; *Uneven* means "rough" or "irregular."

2. if the other team scored a goal, the Hawks would stop trying; Does a company *exist* that can handle this challenge?

3. (mood); A person with a *sulky* expression would frown or look moody.

4. lots of practice and belief in yourselves; *Talented* means "gifted" or "having natural ability."

5. feel her old feeling; *Nervousness* is a state of being worried or anxious.

6. If you lose without trying; It was with *regret* that Sue decided not to attend the meeting.

7. (net); An *arched* object is curved at the top.

8. we like to win games, but that is not the only way to measure victory; *Assured* means "promised confidently."

## Reading Warm-up B, p. 83

Words that students are to circle appear in parentheses.

**Sample Answers**

1. *everywhere;* The colorfully dressed trick-or-treaters marched *throughout* the neighborhood.

2. smells, sounds, and sights; An *assortment* is a variety.

3. Flower markets, red, yellow, pink, and white flowers; My favorite flower is a daisy, and its *petals* are white.

4. the many objects in souvenir shops; *Fascinated* means "bewitched or very interested by."

5. (statues of animals); Other *miniature* objects sold in stores include model cars and dollhouse furniture.

6. *entirely;* The action movie is *purely* entertaining.

7. (of Asian culture); *Images* are pictures, ideas, or likenesses of someone or something.

8. Spicy food may bring about a heaving chest. *Heaving* means "rising and falling, as when breathing."

## Writing About the Big Question, p. 84

**A.** 1. challenge, struggle

2. desire

3. communication, understanding

4. outcome

**B. Sample Answers**

1. My dad really wanted me to join the soccer team, so I did, but my heart wasn't in it and I didn't play well.

2. My dad was disappointed and I was frustrated, but after some honest **communication**, we reached a **compromise**: I joined the cross-country team. During the week, I run with the team, and on weekends I kick a soccer ball around with my dad. We're both much happier.

**C. Sample Answer**

When a person does not live up to someone else's expectations, the loser is the person who has been pressured to meet those expectations. He or she can be made to feel like a failure. Everyone should be encouraged to develop to the best of their ability in the things that interest them. That way, they will feel like winners, and so will the people encouraging them.

## "Two Kinds" by Amy Tan

## Reading: Read Ahead to Verify Predictions and Reread to Look for Details, p. 85

For incorrect predictions, **Event and Detail** follow **Verification:**

2. Correct

3. Incorrect / The daughter performs very badly. The narrator says, "I dawdled over it, playing a few bars and then cheating. . . . I never really listened to what I was playing. I daydreamed."

4. Incorrect / The daughter leaves the piano at her mother's. She says, "Are you sure? . . . I mean, won't you and Dad miss it?"

## Literary Analysis: Characters, p. 86

**A. Sample Answers**

1. stubborn, guilt ridden, angry

2. determined, proud, stubborn

**B.** 1. B; 2. E; 3. D; 4. C; 5. A

## Vocabulary Builder, p. 87

**A. Sample Answers**

1. No, she would not have been, because no one is ever perfect, and to be beyond reproach, one must be perfect.

2. She would have felt as if she had been destroyed.

**Essay**

16. Students should name the two settings as Earth (specifically, the Chicago area) and the planet of Kaan (especially one family's home). They should describe how the people on Earth are fascinated by the horse-spider creatures and how the horse-spider creatures are fascinated by the people on Earth, and they should recognize that the theme of "Zoo" is that when viewing others, people focus on the ways in which they are different rather than on similarities.

Difficulty: *Average*

Objective: *Essay*

17. Students should describe Professor Hugo's colorful cape and his top hat; they might suggest that he dresses like a circus ringmaster. They should realize that he tries to stir up excitement in his audience by telling them to hurry, by declaring that they are getting their money's worth, and by claiming that he has gone to "great expense" to bring them his zoo. By urging his audience to spread the word about his zoo, he is attempting to get free advertising. Students should recognize that the Professor makes money from both the creatures in the show and those who come to see it. Both groups pay him because they are curious about other creatures and other places. Some students might think that because Professor Hugo is not honest, he is taking advantage of those who pay him; others might say that because those who pay him get something for their money, they are not taken advantage of.

Difficulty: *Challenging*

Objective: *Essay*

18. Students should note that the conflict comes from ignorance on both sides: both the Earthlings and the horse spiders think that they need to be protected from each other by metal bars, because they do not realize how similar they are to each other despite the fact that they look so different. In this sense, both the Earthlings and the Kaan creatures are losers, because they create conflict based on ignorance instead of reaching out and understanding each other based on what they have in common: the use of language, curiosity about the unknown, family life, and so on.

Difficulty: *Average*

Objective: *Essay*

## "Ribbons" by Laurence Yep

## Vocabulary Warm-up Exercises, p. 184

A. 1. strapped
2. ankles
3. clumsily
4. wobbly
5. exercises
6. ballet
7. downward
8. beginners

**B. Sample Answers**

1. No; to undo the setting on an alarm is to turn it off, so if you *undid* the setting, you would not wake up on time.
2. No; *mechanical* means "done in a machinelike way," so a mechanical performer would not sing with expression.
3. Yes; something that is *attractive* is pleasing to look at.
4. Yes; a *legal* parking spot is one that is permitted by the law.
5. Yes; *deliberately* means "purposely," so something done deliberately is planned.
6. No; *circulating* means "moving around," so if water is not moving, it is not circulating.
7. Yes; *regained* means "recovered" or "got back to something," so if a runner regained her lead, she was again in first place.
8. No; *illustrating* means "explaining with pictures," so the teacher is not illustrating an idea if she is only talking about it.

## Reading Warm-up A, p. 185

Words that students are to circle appear in parentheses.

**Sample Answers**

1. (form of dance); Ballet is a performance of dance and music that tells a story.
2. when they are between eight and ten years old; Beginners are people who are just starting out with something.
3. (at a *barre*); I do sit-ups and stretching exercises.
4. *upward;* From the balcony, the spectators looked downward at the performers.
5. The shoes are fastened with straps to the part of the leg between the calf and the foot; The model strapped on her sandals and lifted her skirt to reveal her ankles.
6. At first the feet are shaky because the position feels so awkward. Someone who is not used to ice skating might be wobbly.
7. Only with constant practice can a dancer make a performance look easy and graceful; *Clumsily* means "carried out without skill or grace."

## Reading Warm-up B, p. 186

Words that students are to circle appear in parentheses.

**Sample Answers**

1. established itself in Hong Kong; *Deliberately* means "purposely."
2. (Hong Kong); The beautifully kept garden was attractive.
3. (treaty) *or* (agreement); *Legal* means "lawful" or "having to do with the law."
4. Britain's rule of Hong Kong; With the click of the mouse, I undid my mistakes.
5. (control of Hong Kong); *Regained* means "got back to" or "recovered."

6. (an agreement in name only); *Mechanical* means "done in a machinelike way."

7. In Hong Kong, trade and shipping are like the blood circulating through the human body. If someone's blood is circulating poorly, his or her hands and feet might feel cold.

8. The merchants are illustrating Hong Kong's importance as an economic center. A map of Hong Kong would be illustrating the region's location.

## Writing About the Big Question, p. 187

**A.** 1. struggle
2. conflict, competition
3. challenge, struggle
4. communication, understanding, compromise

**B. Sample Answers**

1. When my friend Sondra's grandfather came to live with her family, he criticized her all the time for spending so much time on the computer.
2. Sondra realized the computer was a new and mysterious object to her grandfather, so she taught him how to use it. Now they have a new **conflict**: They **compete** to use the computer!

**C. Sample Answer**

Family members from different generations often do not understand the best way to talk with one another. They may value different things and behave in very different ways and not understand why others don't share their values and behaviors. This can lead to conflict and a breakdown in communication.

## "Ribbons" by Laurence Yep

## Reading: Make Inferences by Reading Between the Lines and Asking Questions, p. 188

### Sample Answers

1. Grandmother is not used to physical affection.
2. Grandmother does not feel at home.
3. Grandmother would rather feel pain than be reminded of the practices of the past.
4. Grandmother is uncomfortable showing affection, but she wants to show that she cares for Stacy.
5. Stacy believes that she and Grandmother are overcoming their differences and discovering how strongly they are connected.

## Literary Analysis: Theme, p. 189

### Sample Answers

1. The setting is a two-story, three-bedroom apartment in San Francisco. (Note that students are unlikely to determine the number of bedrooms.)

2. *Grandmother:* She scolds Stacy for many things: for hugging her; for complaining when Grandmother gives Ian her ice cream; for the ribbons on her toe shoes, which Grandmother says will ruin Stacy's feet; for going into the bathroom when Grandmother is bathing her feet. At the end, however, she explains to Ian the importance of the little mermaid's wish to walk despite the pain that walking causes her.

*Mom:* She explains her mother's behavior to Stacy. She tells her that in China, boys are considered more important than girls. She explains how and why her mother's feet were bound.

*Stacy:* She complains to her mother about her grandmother's behavior. When given the chance, she explains her love of dance to her grandmother and explains that the ribbons are for tying on her dancing shoes, which she loves.

3. *Grandmother:* She ignores or scolds Stacy and pays attention to Ian. Finally, though, she listens as Stacy reads "The Little Mermaid" aloud, and she uses that story to talk about her bound feet. Then, she listens and watches as Stacy explains her love of ballet.

*Stacy:* She tries to show affection for her grandmother by hugging her. She tries to get her grandmother's attention by asking for help with her toe shoes. She gets angry and ignores her grandmother. Finally, though, after her grandmother talks about her bound feet by talking about the little mermaid, Stacy tries again to explain her toe shoes and her love of ballet to Grandmother, and this time she succeeds.

4. The important objects are the satin toe shoes, the silk ribbons, Grandmother's feet, and the fairy tale "The Little Mermaid."

5. The subject is cultural differences.

6. The theme is that cultural differences can be bridged through communication.

## Vocabulary Builder, p. 190

**A.** 1. laborious; 2. exertion; 3. sensitive; 4. coax; 5. meek; 6. furrowed

**B. Sample Answers**

1. She works hard and steadily.
2. A harmonious tune is pleasing because it is full of harmony; a dissonant tune lacks harmony.
3. The child would probably eat large amounts of the great-tasting food.

## Enrichment: Documentary, p. 191

The items that students choose should relate to and have significance in the lives of their subjects. In their commentary, students should write coherently and demonstrate an understanding of the narrative form.

## "Zoo" by Edward D. Hoch
## "Ribbons" by Laurence Yep

## Integrated Language Skills: Grammar, p. 192

**A.** The adverbs to be underlined are followed by the words they modify.

1. slowly—slid; up—slid; how? where?
2. around—clustered; quickly—collected; where? how?
3. quickly—filed; out—filed; how? where?
4. especially—enjoyed; to what extent?
5. formally—bowed; how?

**B.** Sample Answers

1. If I do not <u>move</u> quickly in the morning, I will miss the school bus.
2. I never <u>eat</u> spinach.
3. When I groom my dog, I <u>comb</u> his fur gently.
4. In the summer, I always <u>check</u> the dog for fleas and ticks.
5. Finally, I <u>give</u> the dog a bath.

## "Ribbons" by Laurence Yep

## Open-Book Test, p. 195

### Short Answer

1. Ian shouts excitedly when he first sees his grandmother. Stacy only looks out the window at her. Stacy has had to make sacrifices; she gave up her bedroom and her ballet lessons, so she might resent the arrival of their grandmother. Ian has not had to make any sacrifices, so he greets her more warmly.
   **Difficulty:** *Easy*    **Objective:** *Interpretation*

2. Grandmother is not used to being hugged because that kind of contact is not common in her culture. Such cultural differences can lead to misunderstandings.
   **Difficulty:** *Easy*    **Objective:** *Literary Analysis*

3. Ian does not speak Chinese.
   **Difficulty:** *Easy*    **Objective:** *Reading*

4. She is reminded of the ribbons that once bound her own feet, and she is afraid they are hurting Stacy's feet in the same way.
   **Difficulty:** *Average*    **Objective:** *Interpretation*

5. Grandmother's feet were injured by binding her feet to make her more attractive to men. This shows that women's well-being took a back seat to the desires and interests of men, who thought women with small, bound feet were more attractive.
   **Difficulty:** *Challenging*    **Objective:** *Interpretation*

6. She is ashamed of her feet because they are ugly and deformed, and they show she was hurt as a child so she could be considered beautiful.
   **Difficulty:** *Average*    **Objective:** *Interpretation*

7. Grandmother's comment shows that she cares about Stacy, even though she does not know how to show it.

She doesn't want Stacy to feel the pain and suffering that she experienced from having her feet bound.
   **Difficulty:** *Challenging*    **Objective:** *Reading*

8. Meaning of ribbons for Grandmother: They represent pain and suffering from her old life.
   Meaning of ribbons for Stacy: They represent dancing, which she loves
   Sample answer: The contrasting meanings of the ribbons highlight the theme of cultural differences.
   **Difficulty:** *Average*    **Objective:** *Literary Analysis*

9. Stacy and Grandmother are separated by a big difference in age and cultural backgrounds: Grandmother's love of old customs and her embarrassment about her feet, and Stacy's more informal American ways and her love of ballet. Later, as they learn about each other's backgrounds, they are able to reach across these differences and understand each other.
   **Difficulty:** *Challenging*    **Objective:** *Literary Analysis*

10. Because she is old and because her feet are deformed, climbing stairs is difficult for her, and *laborious* means "very difficult."
   **Difficulty:** *Average*    **Objective:** *Vocabulary*

### Essay

11. Students should note that "The Little Mermaid" serves as a starting point for Stacy and Grandmother to have a conversation about their misunderstanding. The story helps Stacy understand how Grandmother feels about her feet, and it helps Grandmother understand how Stacy feels about dancing.
   **Difficulty:** *Easy*    **Objective:** *Essay*

12. Students might note these cultural differences: Grandmother doesn't understand hugs and dotes on Ian because he is a boy. Stacy reacts first by trying to win her grandmother's affection and then by ignoring her. The two characters are finally able to resolve their differences by talking about them. Students should point out that the story suggests that people must understand and discuss cultural differences in order to understand each other.
   **Difficulty:** *Average*    **Objective:** *Essay*

13. Some students might argue that Stacy is more to blame because it would be easier for her, as a young person, to be flexible about understanding why an older person such as Grandmother might be set in her ways—especially when she has just arrived into a new and strange culture. Others might argue that Grandmother is mainly responsible because an older person should have the wisdom to reach out to younger people. Others might argue that both are responsible—that both are caught up in false pride until they learn how to reach across age and culture to understand the viewpoint of another person.
   **Difficulty:** *Challenging*    **Objective:** *Essay*

14. Students should note that the conflict occurs because Grandmother dotes on Ian and ignores or scolds Stacy. When Stacy learns how Grandmother's feet were bound, and they are able to talk about this and about Stacy's love of ballet, they can understand each other more fully. Students may point out that both characters win the conflict.

**Difficulty:** *Average*    **Objective:** *Essay*

## Oral Response

15. Students should give oral explanations in response to the questions they choose or that are assigned to them.

**Difficulty:** *Average*    **Objective:** *Oral Interpretation*

## "Ribbons" by Laurence Yep

### Selection Test A, p. 198

### Critical Reading

| | | |
|---|---|---|
| 1. ANS: C | DIF: Easy | OBJ: Interpretation |
| 2. ANS: B | DIF: Easy | OBJ: Interpretation |
| 3. ANS: A | DIF: Easy | OBJ: Reading |
| 4. ANS: A | DIF: Easy | OBJ: Reading |
| 5. ANS: B | DIF: Easy | OBJ: Comprehension |
| 6. ANS: D | DIF: Easy | OBJ: Comprehension |
| 7. ANS: C | DIF: Easy | OBJ: Comprehension |
| 8. ANS: C | DIF: Easy | OBJ: Interpretation |
| 9. ANS: A | DIF: Easy | OBJ: Interpretation |
| 10. ANS: D | DIF: Easy | OBJ: Interpretation |
| 11. ANS: B | DIF: Easy | OBJ: Literary Analysis |
| 12. ANS: A | DIF: Easy | OBJ: Literary Analysis |

### Vocabulary and Grammar

| | | |
|---|---|---|
| 13. ANS: B | DIF: Easy | OBJ: Vocabulary |
| 14. ANS: D | DIF: Easy | OBJ: Vocabulary |
| 15. ANS: C | DIF: Easy | OBJ: Grammar |

### Essay

16. Students should recognize that the conflict occurs because Grandmother dotes on Ian and scolds Stacy and ignores her. Grandmother misunderstands the purpose of Stacy's toe-shoe ribbons: She thinks that Stacy is binding her feet with them. Stacy then learns how Grandmother's feet had been bound and are deformed as a result. After Stacy reads "The Little Mermaid," Stacy and Grandmother talk about the mermaid's decision to walk and the challenge that decision presented. Talking about the story's message allows Stacy and Grandmother to talk about Grandmother's feet and Stacy's love of ballet, and that discussion allows them to understand each other better and get along better.

**Difficulty:** *Easy*
**Objective:** *Essay*

17. Students should identify the important objects as Grandmother's feet and the ribbons on Stacy's ballet slippers, and they should recognize that both objects relate to the title of the story. They relate to the theme as well because they represent the cultural differences that separate Grandmother and Stacy. To Grandmother, ribbons represent pain; to Stacy, they represent her passion for ballet. Students should recognize that Grandmother and Stacy demonstrate the theme after Grandmother listens to Stacy read the story about the mermaid. The mermaid learns to walk despite the pain it causes. Grandmother then listens as Stacy explains that the ribbons she'd shown her earlier are used to tie her dancing shoes, not to bind her feet. Therefore, through communication, Stacy and her grandmother overcome their differences.

**Difficulty:** *Easy*

**Objective:** *Essay*

18. Students should note that the conflict occurs because Grandmother dotes on Ian and ignores or scolds Stacy. When Stacy learns how Grandmother's feet were bound, and they are able to talk about this and about Stacy's love of ballet, they can understand each other better, so both characters win the conflict.

**Difficulty:** *Easy*

**Objective:** *Essay*

### Selection Test B, p. 201

### Critical Reading

| | | |
|---|---|---|
| 1. ANS: C | DIF: Average | OBJ: Interpretation |
| 2. ANS: D | DIF: Challenging | OBJ: Reading |
| 3. ANS: C | DIF: Average | OBJ: Literary Analysis |
| 4. ANS: A | DIF: Average | OBJ: Comprehension |
| 5. ANS: A | DIF: Average | OBJ: Reading |
| 6. ANS: D | DIF: Average | OBJ: Comprehension |
| 7. ANS: B | DIF: Challenging | OBJ: Interpretation |
| 8. ANS: A | DIF: Challenging | OBJ: Interpretation |
| 9. ANS: C | DIF: Average | OBJ: Reading |
| 10. ANS: A | DIF: Average | OBJ: Literary Analysis |
| 11. ANS: B | DIF: Challenging | OBJ: Literary Analysis |

### Vocabulary and Grammar

| | | |
|---|---|---|
| 12. ANS: A | DIF: Average | OBJ: Vocabulary |
| 13. ANS: C | DIF: Average | OBJ: Vocabulary |
| 14. ANS: B | DIF: Average | OBJ: Grammar |
| 15. ANS: C | DIF: Average | OBJ: Grammar |

### Essay

16. Students might note these cultural differences: Grandmother stiffens and scolds Stacy when Stacy hugs her. Grandmother favors Ian because he is a boy. Grandmother reacts angrily when she sees the ribbons to Stacy's toe shoes. Students should note that Stacy feels